DR. DONALD J. CLARK

Paranoid Personality Disorder

The Ultimate Guide for Spouses on How to Overcoming Paranoid and Suspicious Thoughts, Understand Symptoms, Treatment, and Prevention of PPD

Contents

Preface

Understanding Paranoid Personality Disorder: A Journey of Compassion and Healing

In the complex landscape of the human mind, there lies a spectrum of emotions, behaviors, and thought patterns that shape our individuality. While this diversity can be a source of wonder and fascination, it can also present significant challenges, particularly when mental health issues are involved. Among these challenges is Paranoid Personality Disorder (PPD), a condition that occupies a unique and often misunderstood space in the realm of mental health. It is a disorder that casts a long shadow over the lives it touches, affecting not only those diagnosed but also their loved ones.

As the author of this guidebook, "Paranoid Personality Disorder: The Ultimate Guide for Spouses on How to Overcoming Paranoid and Suspicious Thoughts, Understand Symptoms, Treatment, and Prevention of PPD," I, Dr. Donald J. Clark, come before you with a heartfelt commitment to making a positive impact on the lives of those affected by PPD. This journey into understanding and addressing PPD is deeply personal for me, inspired by the desire to shed light on a condition often shrouded in darkness and fueled by the hope of facilitating transformation and healing.

The Importance of Understanding Paranoid Personality Disorder

Before we delve into the comprehensive insights and practical strategies presented in this guide, it is essential to recognize the significance of understanding PPD. Mental health issues do not discriminate based on gender, yet the ways in which they manifest can be influenced by cultural, social, and gender norms. This guide explores PPD with an awareness that both men and women may face unique challenges in recognizing, addressing, and seeking help for mental health disorders.

By examining PPD through this nuanced lens, we aim to illuminate a topic that has long been obscured by societal expectations and misconceptions. Understanding PPD is crucial not only for those directly affected but also for their spouses and loved ones, who play a vital role in the journey towards healing and recovery.

My Personal Journey: A Brief Introduction to the Author

Every exploration into the realm of mental health is enriched by the personal experiences and motivations of its guide. Allow me to introduce myself and share the personal thread that weaves through the fabric of this book.

My name is Dr. Donald J. Clark, and my path into the field of mental health has been shaped by both professional and personal experiences. My journey was profoundly influenced by a close friend's struggle with PPD. Witnessing their battle, and navigating the complexities of diagnosis, treatment, and recovery, ignited a passion within me to specialize in understanding and supporting individuals with PPD.

Throughout this book, you will encounter a blend of professional insights and personal anecdotes drawn from my friend's courageous journey. This synthesis of factual information and lived experiences forms the foundation of a holistic understanding of PPD, its impacts, and the steps toward rehabilitation.

A Beacon of Hope and a Roadmap to Healing

This guidebook is more than a compilation of clinical insights; it is a beacon of hope for those ensnared by the labyrinth of paranoia, suspicion, and fear. It offers practical advice, compassionate understanding, and actionable strategies designed to empower spouses and individuals navigating the challenges of PPD. As you turn these pages, you will discover not only the intricacies of Paranoid Personality Disorder but also a roadmap to emotional healing and relationship restoration.

This book is a testament to the transformative power of knowledge, empathy, and unwavering commitment to change. It serves as a guiding light for those affected by PPD, offering tools to foster trust, intimacy, and emotional well-being within relationships.

Joining Hands on the Journey

Let us embark on this journey together, equipped with the knowledge, techniques, and empathy needed to confront Paranoid Personality Disorder head-on. Whether you are a spouse seeking to understand and support your partner, a loved one looking for answers, or an individual grappling with PPD yourself, this guide offers illumination, hope, and a path forward.

In closing, I invite you to join me in unraveling the complexities of PPD, exploring the depths of this condition, and discovering the strategies that can lead to healing and recovery. May this book be your compass, guiding you toward understanding, empathy, and the rekindling of love and trust.

Dr. Donald J. Clark

I

Part One

Unveiling the Mysteries of Paranoid Personality Disorder

This section defines PPD, explores its causes, and distinguishes it from other disorders. It examines the impact on relationships, offers management strategies, and differentiates between natural suspicion and paranoia. We aim to illuminate PPD and provide guidance for those affected.

Chapter 1

What exactly characterizes Paranoid Personality Disorder?

Paranoid personality disorder is a mental health condition characterized by persistent paranoia as well as feelings of mistrust and suspicion toward others. Historically, personality disorders were assumed to be hereditary rather than treatable mental diseases. Personality disorders, on the other hand, are now recognized as a part of the mental health disease spectrum that may be effectively treated.

A person with paranoid personality disorder often feels that someone is intending to harm them, and the condition is diagnosed when paranoia starts to seriously interfere with a person's career, personal, or social life.

Paranoid personality disorder is defined by a maladaptive reaction to stress and life events that influences the sufferer's coping behavior as well as how they perceive and make sense of their surroundings.

Men are more likely than women to suffer from paranoid personality disorder. Long-term and widespread mistrust and suspicion of individuals and their motives impairs a person's ability to build or maintain social and interpersonal connections.

When does paranoid personality disorder start?

People with paranoid personality disorder often develop symptoms and indicators of the condition by late adolescence or early adulthood.

Who is affected by paranoid personality disorder?

Overall, research suggests that those assigned female at birth (AFAB) are more likely to develop paranoid personality disorder (PPD), but those assigned male at birth (AMAB) are less likely to do so.

People suffering with PPD are more prone to:

Live in a low-income home.

You may identify as African-American, Native American, or Hispanic.

You might be widowed, divorced, separated, or unmarried.

More study is required to understand why these risk factors are associated with PPD and how stress and trauma influence its development.

What is the incidence of paranoid personality disorder?

It is unusual to have paranoid personality disorder. According to research, it affects between 0.5% and 4.5% of the US population.

Causes of Paranoid Personality Disorder.

There are no known causes for this condition. However, genetics, familial influences, and traumatic life events may all play a role in the illness's development. Paranoid personality disorder may occur in families with a history of psychotic diseases, such as schizophrenia.

What are the signs of paranoid personality disorder?

People with paranoid personality disorder (PPD) are always on alert, believing that others are attempting to humiliate, harm, or threaten them. Their capacity to build meaningful or even functional relationships is hampered by these often inaccurate assumptions, as well as their blaming and distrusting tendencies. People suffering with PPD have dramatically reduced their social activities.

People with PPD may be skeptical of others' devotion, loyalty, and honesty, fearing they are being used or tricked.

They are hesitant to trust others or provide personal information for fear of it being exploited against them.

Hold grudges and be unforgiving.

Be very sensitive and rude to criticism.

Interpret tiny cues in others' nice comments or relaxed appearance.

They sense assaults on their character that others can not see.

Have persistent, unfounded concerns that their spouses or romantic partners are unfaithful.

To prevent being fooled, they may develop chilly and distant connections with others, as well as control and jealousy.

They refuse to admit their roles in crises or conflicts because they believe they are always correct.

Have difficulties unwinding.

Be combative, stubborn, and argumentative.

Common Characteristics:

Most people with paranoid personality disorder feel that others are deliberately aiming to harm them. They are always scrutinizing people's intentions and integrity, seeking for indicators that someone is trying to hurt them.

Some people with this illness are disagreeable, distant, or aggressive. Those suffering from the condition often exhibit a lack of humor. They may also misunderstand praise and criticism.

They may also be dealing with other mental health disorders including anxiety and depression.

Which factors lead to paranoid personality disorder?

The exact etiology of paranoid personality disorder (PPD) is unclear, however it is most likely caused by a mix of environmental and biological variables.

According to studies, childhood emotional neglect, physical neglect, and supervisory neglect all contribute to the development of PPD in adolescence and early adulthood.

Researchers used to believe that there was a genetic relationship between schizophrenia, schizotypal personality disorder, and PPD, but a recent research found that this association is less than previously assumed.

Diagnosis

Clarifying a patient's paranoid thinking diagnosis is a critical first step in treatment, with consequences for prognosis, therapy, and medicolegal issues including forced treatment or criminal culpability. The DSM-IV-TR criteria for paranoid personality disorder (American Psychiatric Association 2000) have been criticized for failing to capture the illness's normal emotional and interpersonal features, which offer a more full picture of the condition's typical presentation.

The diagnosis is based on long-term evidence that maladaptive components of emotion, thought, and behavior persist, similar to other personality disorders. Collateral data are therefore necessary to demonstrate that the features are not restricted to certain situations (such as therapeutic interactions), but have persisted throughout adolescence or early adulthood.

What are the symptoms of paranoid personality disorder?

Personality develops when a child or adolescent matures. As a consequence, healthcare practitioners often fail to diagnose someone with paranoid personality disorder (PPD) until they reach the age of 18.

Personality disorders, such as PPD, are difficult to diagnose since most persons with these diseases are unaware of their unusual behavior or way of thinking.

When they do seek treatment, it is usually for symptoms caused by their personality disorder, such as anxiety or depression due to divorce or broken relationships, rather of the condition itself.

When a mental health professional, such as a psychologist or psychiatrist, diagnoses a patient with paranoid personality disorder, they often ask broad, general inquiries that do not elicit a defensive reaction or hostile atmosphere. They ask probing inquiries about your background, connections, and professional experience.

- Reality check.
- Impulse control.

Mental health professionals diagnose paranoid personality disorder using criteria from the American Psychiatric Association's Diagnostic and Statistical Manual of Mental Disorders.

Are there any additional medical conditions related to paranoid personality disorder?

Yes, 75% of individuals with paranoid personality disorder (PPD) have another personality disorder. The most prevalent personality disorders that co-occur with PPD are listed below:

- Borderline personality disorder (BPD) is characterized by avoidance and has similarities to antisocial personality disorder (ASPD).

People with PPD are also more prone than the general population to have drug addiction and panic episodes.

The following are the most likely alternate diagnoses.

Normality

When diagnosing a patient with cross-sectional features suggestive of paranoid personality disorder, a normal response to unusual events should always be examined. In general, personality disorders might be thought of as excessive, maladaptive variants on common characteristics. Dimensional analysis, as opposed to categorical analysis, seems to be particularly suited to paranoid thinking: 'One person's paranoia is another person's reasonable caution, and one person's trust is another person's gullibility… Normal growth entails acknowledging that "not everyone who appears trustworthy is trustworthy" (Blaney, Millon, Blaney, and Davis Blaney 1999: p. 343).

Suspiciousness may be adaptive in some contexts, but determining how much interpersonal trust is appropriate in a given setting may be a "vexing judgmental conundrum" (Kramer 1998). Members of minority groups, for example, may engage in defensive reasoning that is legitimate in the wider social context rather than signaling a mental illness.

An epidemiological study of a New Zealand community sample discovered that 12.6% had at least some paranoid characteristics (Reference Poulton, Caspi, and MoffittPoulton 2000), and nearly half of American college students report paranoid thinking experiences (Reference Ellett, Lopes, and ChadwickEllett 2003). As a consequence, many people experience mistrust and suspicion from time to time, but these feelings are not unusual since they are transitory, adaptable, and not very disruptive.

Thus, therapeutically relevant paranoid thinking is best seen as an oversimplified version of a common and adaptive psychological process that, in its natural form, offers an evolutionary advantage by raising others' awareness of potential risks to oneself. Conceptual models that stress continuity (rather than equivalency) with normality may be more effective in engaging people with paranoid personality disorder in treatment.

Different sorts of personality disorders.

Clinical symptoms of several personality disorders may resemble those of paranoid personality disorder.

Schizoid Personality Disorder.

Schizoid personality disorder is characterized by social disengagement. Individuals with the condition, on the other hand, are indifferent to others and prefer not to contact with them, rather than distrustful of them, as in paranoid personality disorder.

Schizotypy is a personality disorder.

This condition is marked by a lack of confidence in others, but it also demonstrates major cognitive and logical flaws that differ from those seen in paranoid personality disorder.

A personality disorder marked by avoidance.

Avoidant personality disorder, like paranoid personality disorder, is distinguished by a degree of mistrust of others and subsequent social withdrawal; however, the avoidant person is much less willing to see malevolence in others; their problem is a lack of confidence and a belief that they will perform inadequately in social situations.

A personality disorder characterized by narcissism.

Narcissistic personality disorder is defined by an overwhelming sense of entitlement and grandiosity. However, paranoid symptoms indicative of paranoid personality disorder may occur under stress (Young, Klosko, and Weishaar Young 2003).

Antisocial conduct is one of the characteristics of personality disorders.

The persistent violation of others' rights is a hallmark of antisocial personality disorder. Individuals with paranoid personality disorder may do harm to others in the name of revenge or as a preemptive strike. However, it may be difficult to distinguish between antisocial people's post-hoc excuses for interpersonally harmful behavior and really paranoid thoughts about the victims' malevolent intentions.

Personality Disorder with Borderline Features.

Individuals with borderline personality disorder may have stress-related paranoid thoughts and wrath, but unlike individuals with paranoid personality disorder, these symptoms may not last.

Co-existing diseases.

Comorbidity is present in more than half of cases with paranoid personality disorder and other personality disorders (Widiger, Trull, Widiger, Frances, and Pincus Widiger 1998). In forensic populations, antisocial personality disorder often coexists with paranoid personality disorder.

Fear of social interactions.

Although anxiety symptoms may present initially in patients with paranoid personality disorder, a full mental state test will reveal the underlying characteristics. There is some overlap with anxiety disorders like social phobia and social anxiety, since both may create social disengagement and concern about how others see you. The important contrast is that paranoid personality disorder is characterized by a belief that bad individuals aim to hurt themselves, rather than a fear of unpleasant future events or public scrutiny. According to one study (Reference Reich and Braginsky, 1994), more than half of persons diagnosed with paranoid personality disorder also have panic disorder.

Depression

The relationship between mood and paranoid thinking is complex. Depressive diseases may generate paranoid symptoms, sometimes with the underlying belief that others' persecution is justified: this is referred to as 'bad-me paranoia' (Chadwick, Trower, and Juusti-Butler, 2005). A comprehensive longitudinal history will distinguish between the disorders; if evident symptoms and indications of a depressive illness exist, they must be vigorously treated before a conclusive diagnosis of paranoid personality disorder can be made.

Delusional condition.

In practice, the most challenging differential diagnosis is delusional illness. Paranoid personality disorder is distinguished by the lack of chronic psychotic symptoms, while delusional disorder is defined by persistent non-bizarre delusions in the absence of other markers of mental disease. However, this paradox begs the question of how to distinguish between illusions and deeply held, unique (also known as 'overvalued') ideas. A key distinction is the extent to which reality testing is impaired: in paranoid personality disorder, individuals can at least consider the possibility that their suspicions are unfounded or that they are overreacting, whereas delusional disorder is likely warranted when beliefs of persecution are held with unwavering conviction, resulting in extensive effects on behavior (Reference Skodol, Oldham, Skodol, and BenderSkodol 2005). To make things worse, delusional disorder may develop gradually or be precipitated by a stressful experience in the context of a sensitive paranoid personality, although this is not always the case (Blaney, Millon, Blaney, and Davis, 1999).

In reality, mental health professionals may disagree on specific cases, and the accuracy with which paranoid behavior may be diagnosed has yet to be objectively demonstrated (Haynes 1986). Similarly, while both disorders appear to be genetically distinct from schizophrenia (Asarnow, Nuechterlein, and Fogelson, 2001; Cardno and Mcguffin, 2006), genetic studies have failed to distinguish delusional disorder from paranoid personality disorder (Winokur, 1985).

This diagnostic issue is part of a larger debate about the boundaries of psychosis, as well as the resurgence of the notion that psychotic symptoms should be viewed as dimensional phenomena on a continuum with normal experiences (Claridge and Claridge 1997; van Os, Hanssen, and Bijlvan Os 2000; Bentall and Taylor 2006).

Strauss' seminal paper (1969) offered four criteria for reaching the threshold of clinical psychotic disorder:

- confidence that the spectacular occurrence is real.
- the extent to which culture and stimuli influence the experience.
- How much time was spent on the experience.
- The experience's impossibility.

Others (Claridge and ClaridgeClaridge 1997) have underlined that the most important distinction is not the intensity of symptoms, but their influence on everyday coping abilities, i.e. the functional impairment they cause.

The distinction is difficult to define, and its therapeutic implications extend beyond academic interest. Except for severe decompensation, people with personality disorders are seldom excellent candidates for forced treatment, and if their conduct leads to offending, they are unlikely to be eligible for a criminal defense based on a lack of criminal guilt. Delusional disorder sufferers, on the other hand, may be eligible for involuntary treatment and may be protected from criminal prosecution if they commit an act as a result of their disease (Bronitt et al., 2005).

Although this difference will never be evident, a painstakingly documented history and chronology of the patient's paranoid thinking, as well as a comprehensive mental state assessment, may be helpful.

Other types of psychotic diseases

Schizophrenic disorders must be included in the differential diagnosis of paranoid personality disorder; the existence of ongoing psychotic symptoms and other indicators of schizophrenia typically clarify the difference. Other mental disorders that might cause paranoid symptoms include:

- chronic organic psychosis, including those caused by dementia;
- Substance-induced psychoses: People with paranoid personality disorder are more likely to misuse substances and develop such illnesses.

- brief reactive psychoses caused by acute stressors: comorbidity may occur, and paranoid personality disorder may increase vulnerability to such brief psychotic episodes (Reference Miller, Useda, Trull, Adams, and Sutker Miller 2001), particularly in the context of acute stress, such as imprisonment, migration, or military induction.

Psychological Procedures
Understanding paranoid cognition and behavior in general may enable doctors to better understand and treat people suffering from paranoid personality disorder. Even while most proposed models have focused on a single process, it seems that several cognitive, behavioral, and social processes are involved, interacting and mutually reinforcing. As a result, the mechanisms discussed below (based on research involving participants with a variety of paranoid disorders) should be interpreted as descriptions of various possible alternative pathways to paranoia, with the relative importance of each changing between and within individuals over time, rather than as exclusive,

competing theories.

Biases in cognition

People with paranoid thinking have an externalizing, personal attributional bias, which leads them to blame others for unpleasant occurrences in their life rather than examining their own possible participation to the situation (Bentall, Corcoran, and Howard Bentall 2001; Bentall and Taylor 2006). The typical self-serving bias, in which negative things are placed on other people, is intensified and warped by prejudice against other people and their perceived malice.

A similar tendency occurs to underutilize contextual information when explaining negative outcomes (Gilbert, Pelham, and KrullGilbert 1988).

According to Bentall and Taylor Bentall (2006), attributional bias is a psychological defense against underlying low self-esteem that occurs when an individual's positive picture of themselves is called into doubt. Although there is some evidence that people with paranoia have poor self-esteem in both clinical and non-clinical populations (Martin and Penn, 2001; Ellett, Lopes, and Chadwick, 2003; Combs and Penn, 2004), the link between self-esteem, paranoid thought, and behavior is complicated.

As previously noted, there is evidence of subgroups with particularly low self-esteem and mood who feel their perceived persecution is justified - 'bad-me paranoia' (Chadwick, Trower, and Juusti-Butler 2005). In such cases, the seeming defense of external attribution of blame may only be somewhat helpful in avoiding sad feelings.

Influential Factors in Information Processing
Contextual, situational attributions often need more information

and cognitive resources than external, personal attributions. When cognitive load increases, people prefer to use external, personal, 'paranoid' attributions as a default alternative (Gilbert, Pelham, & Krull, 1988). This might be connected to the postulated relationship between paranoid illnesses and brain damage (Munro, 1988). Similarly, perceptual defects that restrict access to critical social information, notably decreased hearing, have long been associated with an elevated risk of paranoid thinking (Thewissen, Myin-Germeys, and Bentall, 2005).

Minor functional deficiencies affecting social skills have also been linked to paranoia. Social anxiety and subclinical paranoia have been associated with emotional and social perception impairments (Combs and Penn, 2004).

Deficits in 'theory of mind': the ability to understand the intentions and mental states of others (Kinderman, Dunbar, and BentallKinderman 1998), have also been linked to paranoid thinking. This may make it more difficult to attribute unfavorable social experiences to situational (rather than personal) factors, since an inability to grasp another person's point of view may lead to increased personalizations. For example, if a colleague passes down the street without greeting the individual, failing to see that the colleague may have been concerned with stress (a situational attribution) might reinforce the personal attribution that the colleague is disagreeable.

Paranoid people appear to have an attentional bias that causes them to notice and remember (and thus ruminate on) threat-related information, a processing bias that has been shown in both clinical (Reference Garety and FreemanGarety 1999) and non-clinical (Reference Combs and PennCombs 2004) samples.

Interpersonal interactions.

Certain social settings may aggravate paranoid thinking in 'normal' persons. People with paranoid personalities are more prone to exhibit deviant behavior and thoughts under these circumstances. Certain social situations, according to a model based on a review of such social effects (Reference Kramer 1998), are more likely to be appraised in a way that leads to 'dysphoric self-consciousness,' which leads to hypervigilance and rumination, as well as activation of paranoid cognitive biases and behaviors. These may exacerbate feelings of self-consciousness, resulting in a vicious cycle (Fig. 1). These cycles are more likely given the following situations:

Feeling different from the rest of the social group, for example, because of gender, color, or quantity of experience.

- being judged by others with more influence, such as senior professionals.
- concern for one's social position, as when entering a new organization.

Others (Reference Mirowsky and RossMirowsky 1983; Reference HaynesHaynes 1986) have suggested the possibility of paranoid thinking in settings including

- An unexpected social isolation or loss.
- A substantial disturbance to conventional social networks.
- experience with circumstances in which earlier social skills may be rendered useless, such as immigration or jail.
- Significant sensory impairments.
- True helplessness and victimisation.

Paranoid personality disorder is defined as having long-term features that are obvious even in the absence of such events. Understanding how such events might provoke paranoid thinking, on the other hand, not only aids in predicting when signs of paranoid personality disorder will develop, but it also distinguishes paranoid personality disorder from normal reactions to abnormal circumstances.

Paranoia's downhill spiral

These many cognitive, behavioral, and social processes may become mutually reinforcing, culminating in fatal spirals of increasing paranoia. These processes may make it harder to carry out therapeutic changes.

People with paranoid personality disorder often engage in the self-perpetuating behaviors outlined below.

- It is often possible to unearth evidence of ill intent in at least some people, which is readily interpreted as confirmation that the person was 'right all along' to be suspicious.

Alternatively, if others' acts seem benign, they may be seen as a sham or fraud.

- Proving anything negative, such as that a spouse does not have an affair, is logically impossible. The absence of evidence might be seen as indication of a "cover-up."
- People with paranoid personality disorder are usually socially reclusive and exhibit hypervigilance and suspicion while interacting with others. This may dissuade people from contacting someone who has the illness, making them disagreeable and excluding that person. Such events may exacerbate the individual's concerns while increasing their isolation, creating a self-fulfilling prophesy known

as reciprocal determinism (Haynes 1986).

- Because chronic social disengagement disrupts social input, a paranoid person's worldview may have certain difficulties. It is difficult to learn from experience that individuals can be trusted when there is no interpersonal engagement.

As a consequence, paranoid thinking and behavior may be difficult to overcome, resulting in a self-sustaining, self-defeating cycle (Kramer 1998).

A threat of violence.

People with paranoid personality disorder are more inclined to engage in interpersonal violence because they see other people's acts as hostile. The bulk of study data is based on paranoid characteristics, which generally fall short of a diagnosable paranoid personality disorder and are typically present in combination with other substantial risk factors. As a consequence, although there is convergent evidence that paranoid behaviors do increase

Even after controlling for antisocial and borderline disorder, cross sectional research have indicated that paranoid personality characteristics are linked to histories of both violent (Mojtabai 2006) and antisocial (Berman, Fallon, and Coccaro Berman 1998) conduct. Similarly, high rates of delinquency in teenagers have been linked to paranoid qualities such as feeling mistreated, victimized, duped, and the subject of false rumors (Kr).

A meta-analysis of non-clinical populations (Reference Bettencourt, Talley, and Benjamin Bettencourt 2006) found that the personality trait of high rumination, which is expected in paranoid personality disorder, is associated with a proclivity for aggressive behavior, but only under provoking conditions. This shows that violent behavior in paranoid individuals needs some provocation. However, because of their diverse cognitive and perceptual abnormalities,

Pathways to Violence in Paranoia.

Biases in cognitive processing, emotion regulation, and social information processing are important in current theories of aggression (Anderson and Bushman Anderson 2002). There are many reasons why people with paranoid thinking are more inclined to conduct violence.

Because of their low self-esteem and sensitivity to social status, paranoid people may be driven to perform retaliatory and preemptive violent attacks on others (Berman, Fallon, & Coccaro Berman, 1998). They see the world as hostile and frightening.

They are also more inclined to be distrustful and angry of perceived assaults, ruminating over past wrongdoings perpetrated by others; such grudge-bearing inclinations may enhance their risk of violence. Furthermore, the previously stated "malignant spiral," in which persons with paranoid readily provoke hostility in others by suspicious, unusual conduct, may enhance the probability that they may face genuine hostile behavior from others.

Comorbid disorders are critical for detecting and reducing the risk of violence in a paranoid individual.

The combination of a paranoid tendency to see people as hostile and a lack of internal restrictions against violence (as part of an antisocial personality structure, for example) is especially troubling (Blackburn & Coid Blackburn 1999). When acute mental illness prevails in paranoid personality disorder, decreased inhibition thresholds for aggressive conduct owing to psychotic, mood, or anxiety symptoms may apply (Reference Kennedy, Kemp, and Dyer Kennedy 1992).

Other negative behaviors associated with paranoid personality characteristics include stalking (Reference Mullen, Pathe, and Purcell Mullen
2000), issuing threats (Reference MacDonald MacDonald 1963), and
excessive complaining (Reference Mullen and Lester Mullen 2006).

Treatment For Paranoid Personality Disorder

There have been no randomized controlled studies of any of the
proposed treatments for paranoid personality disorder. Despite
this, the sickness should not be regarded as incurable, and there
is widespread agreement on fundamental criteria for treating the
condition (Reference Gabbard and Gabbard Gabbard 2000; Reference
FaginFagin 2004).

**What are the treatment options for paranoid personality disor-
der?**

Individuals with paranoid personality disorder (PPD) seldom seek
therapy on their own. Typically, they are recommended by family,
friends, or employers.

PPD is most often treated with psychotherapy, which includes
cognitive behavioral therapy (CBT) and dialectical behavior therapy
(DBT). This kind of treatment entails talking with a professional to
control symptoms. Therapy attempts to enhance key coping skills such
as trust and empathy, as well as social interaction, communication, and
self-esteem.

People with PPD often mistrust people, which poses a challenge for
healthcare practitioners since trust and rapport-building are critical
components of treatment. As a consequence, many people with PPD
may reject their treatment plan and even question the therapist's goals.

Generally, healthcare professionals do not suggest medication to treat PPD. If a person's symptoms are severe or they have a co-occurring mental disorder, such as anxiety or depression, anti-anxiety, antidepressant, or antipsychotic medications may be recommended.

PREVENTION

Is it possible to avoid paranoid personality disorder?

While paranoid personality disorder cannot be avoided in most circumstances, therapy may help persons with PPD develop more constructive ways to cope with triggering thoughts and events.

PROGNOSIS AND OUTLOOK

What are the prognosis and next actions for paranoid personality disorder?

The prognosis (outlook) for paranoid personality disorder (PPD) is largely decided by the patient's willingness to accept and comply with treatment. In certain circumstances, talk therapy may assist to reduce paranoia and its impact on daily functioning.

If not treated, PPD may impede a person's capacity to create and maintain relationships, as well as their social and occupational performance. People with PPD are more likely than those without personality disorders to leave their employment early in life.

Furthermore, PPD is one of the most reliable markers of violent behavior in a medical setting. Stalking and excessive litigation (lawsuits) are also linked to PPD.

Fundamental ideas

differential diagnosis and comorbidity.

As previously stated, identifying and treating paranoid personality disorder necessitates taking into account any associated personality disorders and/or mental illnesses.

Goals of Therapy

Bernstein et al. (2007) define proper long-term therapy aims as aiding the patient in:

- accept and recognize their sense of vulnerability.
- improve their feeling of value.
- develop a more trusting attitude toward others.
- express their feelings verbally rather than utilizing negative strategies such as shunning or bullying others.

As with many personality disorders, progress is likely to be slow; some believe it will take at least 12 months to evaluate if treatment is beneficial.

Countertransference

Clinicians should avoid reflexive counterattacks, since they nearly invariably result in disengagement or violence. Instead, they should be wary of underestimating the risk of violence owing to overconfidence or simply denial, particularly with female patients. They should be straightforward and strict when required.

Rejection and sensitivity to authority

It is feasible to engage persons with paranoid personality disorder in meaningful therapy, but utilizing force or trickery is unlikely to be effective. Patients experiencing paranoid symptoms are more likely to be referred to therapy by others rather than themselves. When communication happens, the physician should not raise suspicions.

Administration of boundaries.

Paranoid individuals are more prone to misunderstand a clinician's warmth or words of encouragement as a mask for more malicious purposes, hence using a 'warm' therapeutic style is not recommended. Physical contact, or even sitting too close, should be avoided, and someone suffering from paranoia is likely to need more bodily space than the average person. Group treatment should also be avoided (Gabbard & Gabbard, 2000).

Mood imbalances

If clinical indications of a worsening depressive disorder is present, antidepressant treatment should be considered. Patients who see how their paranoid activities have isolated them may feel genuine grief (and potentially suicide thoughts). Any changes in the patient's mood should be reported to their doctor.

Psychotherapy

Individual supportive dynamic psychotherapy (Gabbard and Gabbard 2000) and schema therapy (Young, Klosko, and Weishaar Young 2003) have both been recommended as therapies for paranoid personality disorder. Individuals with severe personality disorders, especially those with paranoid traits, may benefit in the long term from psychosocial residential treatment in conjunction with psychotherapy (Chiesa and Fonagy Chiesa 2003).

Beck and colleagues' method to cognitive treatment for paranoid personality disorder (Reference Beck, Freeman, Davis, Beck, Freeman, and DavisBeck 2004) might be the most effective for general psychiatrists. The basic concept is that clinical paranoia is a systematized and too broad portrayal of a normal adaptive psychological process. Because the primary cognitive model is one of insufficiency, the first objective of such treatment is to strengthen the person.

In the long term, the inclination to assign blame is brought into question and corrected in order to break the vicious cycles involved. Specific targets may include the belief that people are continually hostile and dishonest, or that one must always be on guard for danger. The practice of 'collaborative empiricism,' in which the therapist and patient evaluate the patient's perspectives in light of objective data, may be successful.

Pharmacotherapy

The role of medicines in pure paranoid personality disorder is unclear. If such disorders are regarded to be on the continuum with delusional disorders (Reference Kendler and Gruenberg Kendler 1982), antipsychotic treatment may be appropriate (Reference Grossman and Magnavita Grossman 2004). However, there are presently no such drugs explicitly approved for this use.

Coexisting issues, such as depression and anxiety disorders, as well as developing psychotic diseases, may need therapy.

A message from the Cleveland Clinic.

It is crucial to identify paranoid personality disorder (PPD) as a mental condition.

Seeking assistance as soon as symptoms appear, like with other mental health conditions, may help to lessen disruptions in a person's daily life.

Mental health professionals may provide therapeutic options to assist people with PPD in controlling their thoughts and behaviors.

Family members of individuals with paranoid personality disorder are often nervous, unhappy, heartbroken, and lonely. If you are experiencing these symptoms, you should prioritize your mental health and seek professional treatment.

Conclusions

Despite the scarcity of scientific data on paranoid personality disorder, it can be seen in a variety of situations, including formerly healthy people who have been subjected to extreme stress, people suffering from mental illness, and those suffering from personality disorders, particularly paranoid personality disorder. Skepticism regarding the intentions of others is natural, particularly in certain social contexts, but it may also be detrimental.

Conflict of Interest

None.

MCQs

1. The following features are incompatible with a pure paranoid personality disorder diagnosis:

Frequent inquiries about a love partner's conduct

I was reminiscing about a coworker's attempt to humiliate the patient two years ago.

Ca has a restricted emotional range during therapeutic interactions.

The patient suspects that a neighbor has frequently broken into his house and injected an odorless poison into his fruit.

A horrible social life.

2. The attributional bias toward self-interest:

is typically pathogenic.

Bis is exacerbated by paranoid personality disorder.

Refers to a tendency to emphasize one's own physiological needs above those of others.

refers to the inclination to attribute positive results to external factors.

E is lacking in paranoid disorders.

3.   The following variables are not associated with an increased likelihood of paranoid thinking:

deafness

A bad mental theory.

As a first-year college student

As a new immigrant.

Maintaining solid social bonds.

4. Some of the most often used therapies for basic paranoid personality disorder include:

The acronym CBT stands for cognitive behavioral treatment.

The abbreviation ECT stands for electroconvulsive therapy.

Antipsychotic medication is supplied involuntarily by injection.

Group Psychotherapy

anxiolytics.

When dealing with people who have paranoid personality disorder, it is helpful to:

Take a calm therapeutic attitude.

Share sensitive details about one's own life.

Avoid suggesting that their fears about others are valid.

Demand that the patient take the medication.

Engage in 'collaborative empiricism'.

Chapter 2

Anonymous story of Someone With Antisocial Personality Disorder (ASPD).

As a child, I generally communicated myself via wrath. Andy is my name, and I'm 33 years old. I've been diagnosed with severe antisocial personality disorder (ASPD).

This is a clinical diagnostic phrase that is synonymous with the terms psychopath and sociopath.

You could have preconceived notions about what it involves, and hence the kind of person I am.

You're not alone in this.

A quick Google search for this diagnosis yields a character-damaging picture of someone without empathy and intending to damage herself, others, or both.

Contrary to popular belief, this does not happen in every circumstance.

This is because my life is not, and should not be, what they state.

This is exactly how it is.

My earliest years.

In 1984, I was born to a woman who had no maternal instincts and ignored all of her children. My biological father had schizophrenia, was addicted to opioids, and ultimately committed himself. When I was just a few months old, social services grabbed me and placed me with a foster home.

I was adopted when I was little over two years old. It's remarkable that I was born into such a loving and caring family. Many individuals look up to their parents, but my parents are particularly impressive. I have never encountered two people as nice and loving as they are.

However, between the ages of seven and ten, I was sexually molested by a friend's older brother. My parents were unable to intervene since they were oblivious of what was going on. I did not tell anybody about it until much later.

Experts say I was genetically predisposed to having an antisocial/psychopathic personality, which was 'activated' by a tough upbringing and later sexual assault.

"I became more aggressive and violent during and after the sexual abuse." As a child, anger seemed to be my only way of expressing myself, despite the fact that I had no memory of any emotions.

Even today, when I reflect on those years, I recall everything vividly but without emotion. This relates to all of my memories from this period, not just the abuse.

The abuse stopped (because we migrated for my father's job), but my conduct worsened, especially throughout my adolescent.

My Adolescence.

I was outraged and aggressive, and my actions led to my dismissal from school. I was also rough with animals.

Despite having many friends and being popular at school, I always felt out of place. That is why, when I became older and understood more about my disease, I was able to detect it.

I visited a 'top' clinical psychologist when I was sixteen. He examined me and, despite my complete honesty, gave me a "certificate of sanity," grinned, and sent me on my way; I remember his face as he said it.

Looking back, it was clear that I was in great danger. Two years ago, I gathered all of my medical records and read what he wrote, what my parents told him, and what my general practitioner recommended.

I'm still shocked that a psychologist with his degree could miss what was there in front of his face.

It's likely that if he hadn't, my life might have taken a different path.

My other reality.

But it didn't, and everything returned to normal. After finishing my A Levels, I started working, but once again under performed.

I lacked a defined life plan and was unclear of my goals. Even after years, I'm still struggling to find clarity.

I have ideas for products and vocations, but since I am often bored, I find it difficult to pursue anything long-term rewarding. People have vocations and goals to which they may dedicate time and resources. That isn't something I can do.

Working as a door supervisor, I saw people who were involved in a variety of illicit activities. I was one of them by the age of 21, when I was convicted of my first robbery. However, I hid this from my friends and family and continued with my life as normal.

This was the first time I was diagnosed with antisocial personality disorder, as I now realize. Surprisingly, despite advising me and writing it down, the doctors failed to alert me.

They prescribed antidepressants and anti-anxiety medicines, which temporarily muted my senses but did not treat the root source of my problem. I was never told of the exact diagnosis.

I was living a parallel life. I was a self-employed computer specialist on the one hand, and a serious criminal on the other. This lasted until I returned to court. My lawyer warned me that I would almost probably wind up in prison.

And I feel this was the turning point. I committed to make long-term changes for myself and my loved ones.

My present circumstance.

My fiancée was pregnant, and if I went to prison, I'd miss my daughter's birth and the first three years of her life. Not to mention the possibility of incarceration.

I was eventually diagnosed with severe antisocial personality disorder while attempting to change myself. I sought treatment because I suspected I had ADHD, which was understandable given my impulsive thrill-seeking and low boredom tolerance.

After receiving my diagnosis, I gained insight into the underlying causes of my behavior, which resulted in a better understanding of why I acted the way I did, making my life easier.

This has not been an easy journey. Since 2011, I've worked in a variety of fields and learned a lot about myself, my personality, my strengths, and my weaknesses.

I doubt that anyone I've met since 2011 thinks I'm odd.

My only distinguishing characteristic (if such a thing exists) is my constant boredom and restlessness.

My mind and body appear to require such intense stimulation that it is almost painful. Since 2011, I've focused on physical activities such as weight and strength training, reading, and puzzles.

I frequently see people sitting in front of televisions and wonder how their minds can be so calm.

I am confident that I will never return to my current life of crime, and I have no desire to. The problem now is deciding what to do next, which I consider every day. However, I am uncertain.

During this time, I also saw a private psychiatrist, with whom I talked about my diagnosis and how I could remain 'psychopathic' while caring for my family.

She stated that, while I can love and sympathize with some of my closest friends, I am completely remorseless in all other circumstances.

My family has been very concerned since they learned about my illness. To be honest, I am undecided about informing them.

After searching Google for the issue, they discovered blogs and forums dedicated to it. All of this implies that I am incapable of loving anyone other than myself, and that any signals I send are only to be abused and used again.

However, I am confident that the majority of research on ASPD has focused on dangerous criminal 'psychopaths' who have been imprisoned for major crimes. While many people, including myself, are neither aggressive nor criminal, we live normal lives.

However, my dissatisfaction with my family quickly subsided. As far as I know, I wouldn't be here without their help and support. I am pleased to have them. Unfortunately, my daily commitment to them demonstrates that what they and others believe about me is inaccurate.

What I've done to address my personality issue… One or two.

Rachel is confident and entertaining. She might be secretive and suspicious as well. She explains how being diagnosed has helped her deal with her illness.

Rachel has borderline and avoidant personality disorder. Her Instagram username is @littlegreenshootproject.

As I grew older, I realized that my horrible emotions were too overwhelming and frightening for others to bear, so I began to hide them. On the outside, I appear to be friendly, confident, and humorous. This isn't a lie, but it's a part of myself that I know is accepted and loved, so it feels safe to show, whereas the other parts of myself are too raw and broken to share. I'm worried that if people find out how wounded I am, they will reject me.

I carry a mental ailment with me wherever I go.

Hiding my feelings on the surface resulted in an aching hole in my chest that grew larger and worse over time.

When things became too difficult for me to handle and I felt people could see through my upbeat facade, I would leave. I've lived in a number of places, moved frequently within them, and belonged to a variety of social groups. Every time I made a shift, I told myself, 'This is it; I'm going to be fine now…this is where I belong,' but the problem is that you can't truly escape yourself.

My mental illness follows me around. It may rest for a while, but emotions, like water, will eventually make their way.

When I got over my rose-colored glasses phase, I'd hide and spend even more time at home, avoiding people and immersing myself in other people's lives via movies and audiobooks.

Last year, I saw a psychiatrist, who diagnosed me with borderline and avoidant/anxious personality disorders. This does not suggest that my personality is faulty; rather, it just indicates that I think, feel, and behave differently than others.

My emotions change significantly, similar to bipolar, but instead of lasting days or weeks, I may go through four or more moods in a single day. These quick changes are often the outcome of my interactions with other people.

There are days when I don't want to get out of bed and am afraid to go outside, but there are also days when I wake up feeling like the best mother and wife in the world, when I'm super organized and make everyone a delicious breakfast, when I walk the kids to school, talk to other parents and teachers, and feel enthusiastic, capable, and inspired.

It just takes someone glaring at me or a text with an unclear tone to make me feel like a scolded child. I felt defenseless, ashamed, and scared all at once. Is this person violent toward me? Is there anything I've done that has made them angry? Is it true that I am a horrible person? All of these thoughts drain me, leaving me exhausted, irritated, and emotionally distant.

Balancing my emotions and energies is difficult since I'm doing things like climbing a mountain, holding a dinner party, and launching a new business all on the same day. Despite these successes, I am fatigued in the morning and want for a week of uninterrupted sleep.

I bravely opted to address and accept my feelings, knowing that the trip had not been simple. However, I am now sensing a determination to face the dread and go nonetheless.

Last year, I had greater anxiety and despair, and I started withdrawing from social activities.

I continued to call my mother and husband for reassurance, and he had to rearrange his work schedule to accommodate me. I started searching for sites where we might live on a boat in Essex, visit my parents in Scotland, or go to Italy.

That was when I made the hazardous decision to stay and deal with my feelings. I did not have an easy life, but I am still alive. I've recently started cognitive analytic therapy with a psychologist, and I'm ready to confront my concerns and do it anyhow.

Going to work used to be troublesome, therefore I often changed employment. But now I work for a really supportive colleague who allows me to work from home on bad days and take time off as needed.

The most recent event included the acquisition of a dog. It inspires me to get up early and spend time outdoors. It's a fantastic way to stay in the present. On my off days, I can go for walks and chat to him.

I'm still hoping things will improve. Last week, I told my therapist that my primary goal is to be as nice to myself as I am to my children. It's tough for me to come out and tell folks the truth, but the experience has been amazing so far. I was concerned about how it might affect my future employment or other opportunities, but I'm just glad I don't have to pretend everything is well, which I consider progress.

Finally, I did not feel so alone.

Catherine's actions seemed more understandable when she learned about avoidant personality disorder.

"What is wrong with you?"

This is the question I've been thinking about my whole life. I had seen enough other people to realize two things: first, that I was not normal, and second, how to behave like one.

Individuals with avoidant personality disorder often have heightened sensitivity to criticism and a constant sensation of being criticized.

It usually worked, but I could see it in someone's expression: "What's up with you?

Avoidant personality disorder is characterized by heightened sensitivity to criticism and a sensation of being observed and examined. I have difficulty socializing because I am self-conscious and careful about how I behave and say things, determined that no one sees who I am.

It is exhausting, but I am most comfortable in groups, which may provide a safe haven.

"I would go ahead and try to restart. By the age of 26, I had lived in six different countries across three continents.

The problem was that I was alone when the ideas started. What had I done wrong? I was going to forensically examine every interaction I'd had that day. What kind of idiot was I? How much did they dislike me? Is anyone aware of my concern? Depression and emotional isolation were unavoidable as a result of this amount of self-analysis and self-loathing. I convinced myself that my friends disliked me and that I was better off without them. I'd try again.

But I couldn't keep up with myself.

I eventually arrived in Barcelona and found people with whom I felt at ease, but I kept my fear of emotional attachment with extensive drug use disguised.

That way of living couldn't endure forever, and as the drugs' effects faded, I pondered where those emotions of intimacy had gone and if they were true; I was still alone.

My friends began to marry, which made my avoidance more difficult to hide.

I was 36 years old, had no important relationships in my history, and had a job that required me to avoid interviews and connect with coworkers. I was weary of having to hide who I was, and I felt unfairly evaluated for my bad life performance.

My sleep was broken; when I awoke, it seemed like I had fallen down a stairway.

This eventually got the best of me, and by my mid-thirties, I was exhausted. Over the next few months, my sleep was disrupted, I awoke feeling thrown down a flight of stairs, and my energy fluctuated from day to day and hour to hour. After months of testing, I was diagnosed with chronic fatigue syndrome (CFS).

I was heartbroken.

Even among medical professionals, chronic fatigue syndrome is commonly misunderstood, and I was informed by doctor after doctor that my condition did not exist, which was the worst thing that could have happened to me. I was already feeling convicted and reprimanded, and things were about to become worse.

So I raced off again.

I was unable to adjust to my new living circumstances; everyone was casting judgment on me, and I felt more alone than ever before. I opted to go to Bali because I feared I would have no one to turn to.

Despite seeking respite in support groups for chronic tiredness, anxiety, and depression, none of them related with my feelings. My condition, loneliness, and unhappiness remained unexplained, as did my difficulty connecting with others.

The overpowering sense of loneliness grew as it seemed that no one understood the extent of my isolation.

But I persisted, watching mental illness documentaries, listening to podcasts, and reading blogs, till I came across avoidant personality disorder (AvPD) and burst into tears. I investigated every symptom on the diagnostic criteria!

For the first time in my life, I did not feel lonely, and I began to believe that there was nothing wrong with me; I had a mental illness.
  "I still feel judged, but I know why: my sickness.

Understanding my limits as a result of my disability helped me accept myself. I used cognitive behavioral therapy to help me control my negative self-talk, spoke with my therapist about my social issues and how to deal with them, and participated in a 12-step codependency program. Joining Coda (Co-Dependents Anonymous) and having a safe space to discuss and share my story with others, allowing them to see me at my most vulnerable, was a major stride forward that I could not have anticipated. I still feel judged, but I can explain it as the outcome of my illness and refuse to accept it.

I'm still in Bali, but this time by choice. I am gradually becoming stronger till I am ready to return. The difference now is that I have folks I can consider friends. I do not feel alone since I have emotional support. Slowly, I'm rekindling relationships that I'd abandoned, and I'm beginning to feel that I, too, can have a life.

My OCPD therapy involves painting.
  Emily, who has obsessive-compulsive disorder, discusses how Zentagling helps her.

When I tell people I have OCPD, they think I'm pronouncing it wrong; few people are acquainted with the term. Obsessive-compulsive personality disorder (OCPD) lacks flexibility; rules are rules, and there is minimal room for mistake; nonetheless, consider obsessive-compulsive disorder (OCD) tendencies.

Persons with OCD are often aware that their compulsions and obsessions need treatment, but those with OCPD frequently believe their conduct is normal. With OCPD, I believe that my method is the only way to proceed. All chores, great and little, must be accomplished exactly as I need; otherwise, they are unfinished.

Then comes OCD, which manifests as intrusive thoughts and compulsive repetitive actions. It's simply one big circle.

I understand that it seems that I am being 'picky,' but this is not true.

It's a difficult sickness to convey since it's more like a way of life. OCPD is difficult to identify and manage since it is so firmly ingrained in my thinking.

I also have generalized anxiety and social phobia, so my mind is always racing, even while I am sleeping.

Assume you have 100 tabs open on your internet browser, each displaying your issue. Consider pop-ups that keep appearing and adding new tabs to the ones you already have open; then one starts playing music and another starts playing a video, and you have no clue which tabs are making noise or how to stop them no matter how hard you try. So you're anxiously attempting to determine which tabs are playing the music and video, all as fresh pop-ups arrive in your browser tabs! That is my brain's continual state. Every day, all day.

A wish for relieve

To relax, I started doodling and found my love for Zentangle. I'm a Zentangle artist who taught herself. It's peaceful, and I can't fathom without sketching or painting every day.

Zentangle is just a kind of doodling. The patterns and lines appear as soon as I put pen to paper. I continue painting until I have covered the whole page and my artwork comes to life.

"Before I know it, I've finished a piece of work and felt a bit relieved.

I begin by sketching the basic contour of whatever I'm working on, which might be anything from a coffee cup to an animal or a landscape. Then I use acrylic paint to make a basic color canvas, which looks like large chunks of random colors arranged on a piece of paper. Finally, I add the Zentangle detail!

In addition to sharing some of my artwork on Instagram, I was able to find consolation in the hour or two it took me to complete a work of art.

How Zentangle Can Help You Save Yourself.

Every day, Zentangle saves me from myself by allowing me to freely express myself on paper. The patterns in Zentangle artwork may be addictive, and I get engrossed in the fascinating cognitive process of sketching and painting.

You may be wondering how someone with OCPD handles this kind of art. Isn't it necessary to be precise? No, not with art, and even less with Zentangle. That's the allure of it. Yes, I've thrown away a lot of work because it wasn't quite right, but it doesn't have to be flawless. In reality, it should just be unique and expressive, which is fantastic for someone like me because if I make a mistake, I can easily transform it into another design.

My artworks create a feeling of bustle and intricacy at first look, reflecting my own multifaceted personality.

My artworks, like mine, are complicated and seem tough at first look, yet they provide me with some relaxation from my too-busy mind. Drawing is my kind of therapy.

I am complicated and wonderful, just like anybody suffering from a mental illness, and this is something we must constantly remember.

Chapter 3

In a relationship, how do you manage with paranoid personality disorder?

Unwarranted suspicion, envy, and feelings of persecution by others may emerge from paranoid personality disorder. This might have an affect on many types of interactions. People may handle applying a variety of approaches.

A mental health problem that influences an individual's ideas, emotions, and actions is known as paranoid personality disorder. People suffering from paranoid personality disorder may develop mistrust and suspicion of others. It may induce emotions of persecution in the absence of a danger.

The powerful sensations and ideas that paranoid personality disorder may produce might harm relationships with family, friends, and the workplace. Learning how to deal with a relationship's condition may enhance support and better communication.

This chapter addresses paranoid personality disorder, how it influences relationships, and how to manage with it.

Individuals suffering from paranoid personality disorder may experience the following symptoms:

- a significant skepticism of others • slowness to confide in others and the expression of unforgiveness • sensitive to perceived criticism • a predisposition to stay distant in relationships

Find out more about the paranoid personality disorder.

What consequences does paranoid personality disorder have on relationships?

Relationships might suffer as a result of paranoid personality disorder. Approximately 75% of persons with paranoid personality disorder also have another personality condition, according to Trusted Source.

This combination of personality problems may make maintaining relationships even more problematic.

Depending on the nature of the relationship, paranoid personality disorder may cause paranoid symptoms including intense distrust and suspicion. It may make someone assume, without justification, that their personal connection is unfaithful.

Individuals suffering with paranoid personality disorder may struggle to open up and communicate sensitive details. This may inhibit the creation of genuine friendships or love bonds.

Others' innocent actions and remarks may be misunderstood as a result of paranoid personality disorder. This may lead to stress in many forms of relationships, including those with coworkers.

How to manage with a loved one who suffers from paranoid personality disorder

There are several techniques to manage with and help a loved one suffering from paranoid personality disorder or analogous mental health challenges. It is vital to remember that everyone is unique and that healing is a continuous process.

Clear communication

Clear communication is a vital first step in enabling someone to cope. Being short and straightforward contributes in the reduction of misunderstanding, which may lead to mistrust. Clear communication also aids in the defining of expectations and restrictions.

Recognize their sentiments.

Feelings are genuine to someone suffering from paranoid personality disorder. According to the National Alliance on Mental Illness (NAMI), understanding the person's sentiments while simultaneously striving to redirect their anxieties is useful. Respecting another person's sentiments might assist in de-escalating a situation and ease worries.

Try not to quarrel with them or ignore their opinions.

It is not good to acquire paranoid beliefs. At the same time, challenging and opposing ideas and thoughts is usually fruitless. Using an aggressive approach may just intensify your anger and paranoia.

Establish borders

Even if they are a loved one, it is necessary to develop boundaries with someone who has paranoid personality disorder. Setting boundaries allows a loved one to accept responsibility for their behavior and understand what is expected of them. It may also foster a feeling of independence.

Self-care is crucial.

It is vital to exercise self-care. Finding techniques to relax, unwind, and recharge allows someone to better aid a loved one. The American Psychiatric Association (APA) offers the following self-care measures:

remaining in touch with family and friends often for fun and support

practicing a form of relaxation, such as yoga, meditation, or breathing exercises

Regular exercise, which is a good method to decrease stress and help someone feel better attempting to get enough sleep, since lack of sleep may make it more difficult to deal with stress

What factors contribute to paranoid personality disorder?

The true roots of paranoid personality disorder are uncertain, yet below are numerous plausible explanations of paranoia.

1. biological components

According to study, our genes are responsible for various features of our personality. Genetics, according to specialists, may have an impact on the development of a paranoid personality syndrome.

According to the above-mentioned research, paranoid personality disorder is a repeated recurrence in families with a history of psychosis.

It is not apparent that such illogical conduct is transmitted down genetically to future generations, but it is quite possible.

2. Injuries to the brain

According to studies, there may be a relationship between brain damage and the development of a paranoid personality condition. Following a brain injury, some persons have an increase in paranoia.

3. Other variables

While genetics have a bigger influence, the environment in which a person grows up also plays a vital part in the development of a paranoid personality disorder. Childhood trauma, parental neglect, bullying, or molestation may all have a poor influence on mental health to the point where a person develops paranoid personality disorder over time.

What influence does paranoid personality disorder have on relationships?

It's challenging to love someone who has a paranoid personality condition. It has its own set of obstacles, and you must know how to deal with a deluded individual to keep the relationship strong.

Here's how paranoia effects relationships.

1. The paranoid individual may struggle to trust their spouse and may seek unneeded confirmation of their location from anybody.
2. A paranoid individual may be unduly critical and brutally criticize their partner.
3. They may also wind up hurting their spouse's emotions as a result of their lack of sensitivity, and they may blame their partner for it.
4. They may recall every detail of your actions and hold animosity against you.
5. They may have an overall bad attitude toward their spouse and their relationship. With their spouse, they may engage in passive-aggressive acts.
6. They may desire to have entire control over their relationship and their lives. They may order you to break all communication with friends and relatives.

5 ideas for managing with a paranoid spouse

If you live with someone who has just been diagnosed with paranoia, recognize that the journey ahead will not be straightforward. There will be times when you want to walk away from everything, and others when you simply cannot because others rely on you.

Your patience will be challenged again and again under such harsh conditions. So, how can you help someone suffering from paranoia? Here are five ideas for dealing with a paranoid spouse.

1. Encourage and help them in their pursuit of narcotics.

Once you've learned that your partner is suffering from paranoia, it's crucial to understand how to manage someone who is paranoid.

Please tell them to obtain medical treatment to enhance their lives. It may be tough for them to trust physicians and resist prescriptions, but you must persuade them for their benefit.

Always be there for them and be there for them at all times. With this ailment, early identification and treatment may make life easier and more joyful.

2. Establish precise restrictions in your partnership.

This disease is distinguished by mistrust, skepticism, and continuous suspicion.

This may cause you emotional distress, and you may regularly find yourself on the edge of your relationship.

To prevent such disagreements, it is vital to establish restrictions. This is how you control paranoid allegations.

Consult an expert and go over the limits with them. This will prevent your spouse from mistreating you under the pretense of paranoia.

3. Enhance your communication skills

You may not know it, although every day we say phrases that are vague or baffling.

We figure it out when we start living with a paranoid individual. As a result, to prevent disputes or create their paranoia, you must establish the habit of communicating, correctly, and in non-ambiguous manner.

Following this can help you in preserving a close connection with your spouse while preventing their problem from affecting you.

View this video to understand how to increase your communication abilities.

4. Be alert of probable triggers.

If you want to know how to cope with a delusional spouse or a paranoid partner, you need first to uncover what motivates them to act in this manner. Observe the events that worsen their symptoms and endeavor to avoid them.

Instead, concentrate on their expertise and amazing attributes. You must consider the risk that they do not understand how to cope with paranoia.

5. Begin to emphasis a healthy social life and self-care.

Self-care is vital for every one of us, yet we usually take it for granted. When you live with a paranoid individual, it's time to start paying attention. Begin with self-care and urge your spouse to follow suit. This will allow you to surround yourself with good energy, and you will both feel better as a result.

Similarly, paranoid persons strive to distance themselves from their environment because they feel others are untrustworthy. This may be prevented if you both take little steps toward a healthy social life.

Devote substantial time to your family and intimate friends, producing a sense of actual concern from individuals outside your immediate group for your spouse.

Takeaway

We never know what the future has in store for us. Things might take a radical shift and flip upside down, leaving us perplexed. In such circumstances, we have two choices: flee or face it. However, when it comes to our loved ones, we cannot abandon ship and must solve the problem. When you're in a relationship with a paranoid spouse, this is what occurs. Follow the recommendations on how to cope with a paranoid spouse, and things will improve for you.

Commonly Asked Questions

The following are answers to some often asked questions concerning paranoid personality disorder.

What factors contribute to paranoid personality disorder?

In this 2017 study various studies, according to Trusted Source, have established childhood trauma as a risk factor for paranoid personality disorder. This trauma may entail emotional and physical maltreatment as a youngster.

How can you calm someone who suffers from paranoid personality disorder?

What works best for each individual vary. However, being a good listener, having a caring attitude, and retaining a calm voice and manner may all assist in calming a person.

Which personality problem is the most difficult to treat?

Opinions among doctors dispute on the most challenging personality disorder to treat, and the strength of symptoms may vary from individual to individual. Conversely, some personality problems are generally more resistant to successful treatment.

One of the most hardest disorders to cure is paranoid personality disorder Trusted Source. Furthermore, antisocial personality disorder is difficult to cure, according to the Substance Abuse and Mental Health Services Administration (SAMHSA).

For more Clarity Check out These Books as Well
   Paranoid Personality Disorder: The Ultimate Guide for Spouses on How to Understand Symptoms, Treatment, and Prevention of PPD. By Dr. John E. Collins

Complete Dating Advice Guide for Insecure Couples on How to Cope with a PPD Partner by Dr. John E. Collins

Chapter 4

Is this just my paranoia, or is he lying? 11 Things to Check and Consider.

Trust is one of the most fundamental aspects of a strong romantic relationship. However, if issues like adultery arise, the partnership may end.

You may doubt your partner's actions, only to discover that your assumptions were erroneous. This article will answer the question "Am I paranoid, or is he cheating?"

What's the difference between paranoia and suspicion?

Suspicion and paranoia are sometimes used interchangeably. They do, however, express several meanings. Paranoia is an extreme kind of suspicion in which a person has unfounded concerns of being duped.

Anxiety, depression, and unfounded dread are all signs of paranoia, and they may interfere with a person's daily life. In contrast, suspicion is a normal sense of distrust or doubt about another person's trustworthiness or accountability. When you see disparities in someone's behavior, the natural response is suspicion.

11 signs he's cheating or you're being suspicious

You may have feelings for someone, yet you see signs that he is disloyal to you. Here are some suggestions to help you answer the question: Is it just me, or is he committing adultery?

1. He conceals his phone from you.

When your lover hides his phone, this is one of the most typical answers to the question, "Am I crazy or is he cheating?" If he often changes his password or dislikes having you look at his phone, he may be hiding something from you.

He may not be cheating if you have access to his phone and he doesn't protest.

2. He is more discreet.

If you keep asking yourself, "Why do I suspect he's cheating?" You could learn more about how he arranges his activities. When a man cheats in a relationship, he is very discreet in his activities, so you don't notice.

If he isn't cheating, you may be unaware of his actions since he isn't compelled to divulge them.

3. He keeps an emotional distance.

Assessing his emotional availability is another way to address the question "Am I paranoid, or is he cheating?". If you see that he is not emotionally available and looks preoccupied with his world, you should speak with him to figure out why and develop a solution.

4. He won't say where he is.

The notion of responsibility may be utilized to answer the question "Am I paranoid, or is he cheating?" Partners must be accountable to one another, regardless of where they are.

If your boyfriend finds no motive to tell you of his whereabouts, he might be cheating on you. In contrast, if he notifies you but forgets every now and again, it may be unintentional.

5. He flirts with people on social media.

Cheating is when a guy flirts with other potential partners while remaining in a relationship. Not everyone knows the difference between friendship and unfaithfulness in relationships.

When you see him flirting with other people, you worry whether you're crazy or if he's cheating.

6. Your sex life has taken a plunge.

When you don't want to be sensually personal with your lover, you can worry whether you're angry or if he's cheating on you. If your partner cheats on you, he may deny having sex with you.

Another reason your sex life isn't as joyful as it might be is if your darling is experiencing difficulties and does not want to have sex.

Watch this video to discover how to enhance your sex life.

7. You have more unsolved conflicts.

If you're struggling with several difficulties in your relationship that are getting more difficult to settle, it might be a sign of infidelity. When both partners are devoted to the success of their relationship, they confront conflicts head-on. If your boyfriend seems disinterested in making the relationship work, he may be cheating.

8. He is easily upset.

If your male repeatedly reacts negatively when questioned, "Is my boyfriend cheating?" Even if you do not accuse him of anything, he will react swiftly.

It is important to recognize, however, that individuals may be defensive for a number of reasons, especially if they feel misunderstood or see a possible assault or danger. This validates my concerns that he's cheating on me.

9. Communication breaks down.

Infidelity is not always caused by a breakdown in communication between couples. Job stress, communication style issues, and other variables may all contribute to communication challenges.

As a consequence, while answering the question, "Am I paranoid, or is he cheating?" You must speak with him and develop a communication plan.

10. He obsesses about his appearance.

Individuals who have pondered, "What's making me suspect my partner of infidelity?" They may have seen their significant other concentrate on their own looks. If your spouse is becoming more concerned about their looks, this may not suggest cheating.

Some individuals are self-conscious about their looks in an attempt to boost their self-image or self-esteem. It is normal to question his motives if he is always worried about his looks while meeting individuals who may represent a danger to your relationship.

11. He withdraws from your loved ones.

The way he handles your loved ones will indicate if you are too worried or he is cheating. When men cheat, they may withdraw from their families and friends. However, there is insufficient evidence to establish your dismissal.

Raymond Hoek's book Red Flags outlines the different signs that your boyfriend or girlfriend is cheating on you.

The young wife is cunning and jealous.

What do you do if you discover he's cheating?

Here are some next measures to take if you suspect your partner is cheating on you.

Make no rash choices.

Be careful not to make judgments that will have an influence on you. Allow yourself some time to comprehend the situation and avoid disregarding other elements of your life because of your unfaithful spouse.

Self-care is essential.

Do not blame yourself for your man's adultery. Take a minute to relax and enjoy the experience.

Recognize your emotions, but don't dwell on them.

When you discover your partner is cheating, don't ignore your feelings, but don't let them consume you. Discover effective ways to redirect your attention.

Consult with trusted friends and family.

If you are feeling overwhelmed by what has happened to you, speak with a trusted loved one. It is beneficial to have a support system accessible while you work through the situation.

Seek advice from an experienced relationship counselor.

Consult a relationship therapist or counselor for help on what to do once you realize your partner has cheated on you.

Caroline Madden's book Fool Me Once offers valuable guidance to women suffering with unfaithful partners.

Frequently asked questions.

Here are some questions and answers to help you deal with the challenging topic of infidelity in partnerships. Take a look.

Is he disloyal, or am I just letting my concerns take over? What approaches may be utilized to determine the truth?

If you believe your spouse is cheating, check for symptoms such as a change in behavior, decreasing closeness, a lack of transparency, a sudden shift in routine, and so on. However, some of these indications may appear unintentionally.

Is my partner cheating on me, or am I being unduly paranoid?

whether you have an open and honest chat with them, you will be able to tell whether she is cheating or suspicious. It is fine to be aware of possible cheating indications, but they should not be used to make significant judgments.

How does a guy behave when he cheats?

When a guy is accused of cheating, the issue becomes, "Is he lying to me, or am I being paranoid?" May be raised. When a guy cheats, he may become emotionally isolated and secretive. When confronted with his actions, he may become aloof and defensive.

Why does my partner seem to be cheating on me?

If you feel your partner is cheating on you, do not accuse him of anything. Consider engaging in a non-accusatory discourse with your spouse. Listen without interrupting, and request clarification if needed.

Take an educated judgment.

Have you ever thought, "Am I paranoid, or is he cheating?" This post will address what you should do if you feel your spouse is cheating. Some couples may make the mistake of explicitly accusing their spouses, only to later realize that they were too anxious.

As a consequence, always do your own research and seek advice from a skilled counselor before trying to find the truth on your own.

II

Part Two

Navigating Thought Patterns and Relationship Dynamics in Paranoid Personality Disorder

This section explores the cognitive and behavioral aspects of PPD, distinguishing it from similar disorders, and delves into effective strategies for managing relationships with affected individuals. By understanding these thought patterns and their impact, we provide practical insights and tools to support healthier relationships and personal well-being.

Chapter 5

Analyzing Patterns of Thought Within Paranoia

As with other personality disorders, the diagnosis is based on the existence of maladaptive emotional, cognitive, and behavioral components across time. As a result, supporting data is required to demonstrate that the attributes persist throughout adolescence or early adulthood and are not limited to a single environment (for example, therapeutic encounters).

The most likely alternate diagnosis are as follows.

Normality

When identifying a patient with paranoid personality disorder based on cross-sectional qualities, it is always important to include their natural sensitivity to odd situations. In general, personality disorders may be thought of as exaggerated, maladaptive versions of typical characteristics (Widiger, Frances, Costa, and Widiger 2002). "One person's paranoia is another person's reasonable caution, and one person's trust is another person's gullibility…," as the proverb goes, implying that dimensional analysis, rather than category analysis, is appropriate for paranoid thought. According to Blaney, Millon, Blaney, and Davis (Blaney 1999: p. 343), learning that "not everyone who appears trustworthy is trustworthy" is an important part of growing up. Knowing how much trust to have in others depends on the circumstances, which may be a "vexing judgmental conundrum" (Kramer 1998). Minority members, for example, may engage in defensive reasoning that is acceptable in the larger social context rather than diagnosing a mental disease (see below).

An epidemiological study of a New Zealand community sample revealed that 12.6% had at least some paranoid characteristics (Reference Poulton, Caspi, and MoffittPoulton 2000), and nearly half of American college students report paranoid thinking experiences (Reference Ellett, Lopes, and ChadwickEllett 2003). As a result, many people experience mistrust and suspicion; nonetheless, such attitudes persist because they are transient, flexible, and not very destructive.

Thus, clinically relevant paranoid thinking is best understood as an oversimplified form of a regular and flexible psychological process that serves some evolutionary purpose by making it easy to sense hazards to oneself from others. Therapy for paranoid personality disorder may benefit from conceptual models that see normalcy as a continuum rather than an equivalency.

Personality problems come in numerous kinds.

Clinical signs of several personality disorders may resemble those of paranoid personality disorder.

Schizoid Personality Disorder

Social disengagement is a characteristic of schizoid personality disorder. Individuals with the condition, on the other hand, are uninterested in other people and prefer not to interact with them, as opposed to being scared of them, as is the case with paranoid personality disorders.

Schizotypy is one of the personality disorders that exist.

This condition is distinguished by a level of distrust toward others, but it also exhibits significant cognitive and reasoning mistakes that differ from those exhibited in paranoid personality disorder.

A personality trait characterized by avoidance.

Avoidant personality disorder, like paranoid personality disorder, is characterized by a degree of mistrust of others and subsequent social withdrawal; however, the avoidant person is much less willing to see malice in others; their problem is that they lack confidence and believe they will perform inadequately in social situations.

A personality disorder marked by narcissism.

The overwhelming sense of entitlement and grandiosity that characterizes narcissistic personality disorder. Stress may trigger paranoid personality disorder symptoms.

Antisocial behavior is a sign of a personality disorder.

The repeated violation of the rights of others is an important component of antisocial personality disorder. Individuals with paranoid personality disorder may do harm to others in vengeance or as a preemptive strike. However, distinguishing between antisocial people's post-hoc justifications for their interpersonally destructive behavior and legitimately obsessive views about the victims' evil intent may be difficult.

Personality Disorder with Borderline Features

Stress-related paranoid ideation and wrath may develop in those with borderline personality disorder, although they may not stay as long as those with paranoid personality disorder.

Coexisting diseases.

Comorbidity accounts for more than half of all cases of paranoid personality disorder and other personality disorders. In forensic populations, antisocial personality disorder is often associated with paranoid personality disorder.

Concern about social situations

Although anxiety symptoms may appear as a result of paranoid personality disorder at first, a thorough mental state test will reveal the underlying paranoid core characteristics. There are some similarities with anxiety disorders such as social phobia and social anxiety, since both may cause social disengagement and concern about how others see you. The fundamental difference is that paranoid personality disorder is characterized by dreadful people wanting to harm themselves rather than a fear of unpleasant future events or public scrutiny. According to Reich and Braginsky (1994), more than half of those with paranoid personality disorder also have panic disorder.

Depression

The correlation between mood and paranoid thinking is complicated. Depressive diseases may cause paranoid symptoms, usually with the underlying theme of being persecuted by others; this is known as 'bad-me paranoia' (Reference Chadwick, Trower, and Juusti-Butler Chadwick 2005). A comprehensive longitudinal history may help to distinguish the disorders; if obvious symptoms and signs of a depressive illness are present, they must be aggressively treated before a definitive diagnosis of paranoid personality disorder can be made.

The state of delusion

In practice, the most difficult differential diagnosis to make is delusional sickness. Delusional disorder is defined by persistent non-bizarre delusions in the absence of other signs of a psychotic disease, while paranoid personality disorder is distinguished by the absence of chronic psychotic symptoms. This contradiction, however, raises the question of how to distinguish illusions from strongly held, distinctive (sometimes referred to as 'overvalued') views. The degree to which reality testing is impaired is a key distinction: individuals with paranoid personality disorder can at least entertain the possibility that their suspicions are unfounded or that they are overreacting, whereas delusional disorder is likely warranted when beliefs of persecution are held with incorrigible conviction, resulting in extensive effects on behavior (Skodol, Oldham, Skodol, and Bender, 2005).

To complicate matters further, delusional disorder may develop gradually or be precipitated by a stressful experience in the context of a sensitive paranoid personality, however this is not always the case.

In reality, mental health professionals may disagree on certain instances, and the precision with which persons who exhibit paranoid behavior may be recognized has yet to be objectively demonstrated (Haynes 1986). Similarly, despite the fact that both disorders appear to be genetically distinct from schizophrenia (Reference Asarnow, Nuechterlein, and FogelsonAsarnow 2001; Reference Cardno and McguffinCardno 2006), genetic studies have failed to distinguish delusional disorder from paranoid personality disorder.

This diagnostic issue is part of a larger debate about the boundaries of psychosis, as well as a resurgence of the notion that psychotic symptoms are best conceptualized as dimensional phenomena on a continuum with normal experiences (Reference Claridge and ClaridgeClaridge 1997; Reference van Os, Hanssen, and Bijlvan Os 2000; Reference Bentall and TaylorBentall In his seminal work, Strauss (1969) offered four criteria for determining the threshold into clinical psychotic

- confirmation that the excellent experience was accurate.

- the extent to which culture or stimuli alter the experience
- the time spent on the experience.
- The experience is impossible.

Others have emphasized that the most important distinction is the impact of symptoms on daily coping abilities, or the functional damage they cause.

The variation is modest, but it has therapeutic implications that extend beyond academic curiosity. With the exception of severe decompensation, people with personality disorders are seldom candidates for compulsory treatment, and if their behavior leads to offending, they are rarely eligible for a criminal defense based on lack of criminal culpability. Delusional disorder patients, on the other hand, may be eligible for involuntary treatment and may be deemed to have no criminal culpability if they commit a crime as a result of their illness .

Although this difference may never be obvious, a meticulously documented history and chronology of the patient's paranoid thinking, as well as a thorough mental state evaluation, will be helpful.

Other symptoms of psychotic disorder.

Schizophrenic disorders must be examined in the differential diagnosis of paranoid personality disorder; the presence of persistent psychotic symptoms and other signs of schizophrenia will usually make this distinction clear. Other mental illnesses that may cause paranoid symptoms include:

- persistent organic psychoses, such as those associated with dementia;
- Substance-induced psychoses: people with paranoid personality disorder are more likely to abuse drugs and develop these disorders.

- brief reactive psychoses caused by acute stressors: comorbidity may occur, and a paranoid personality disorder may predispose to such brief psychotic episodes (Reference Miller, Useda, Trull, Adams, and SutkerMiller 2001), especially in the context of acute stressors such as imprisonment, migration, or military induction.

Psychological Approaches

Understanding paranoid cognition and behavior in general may help doctors better understand and treat patients with paranoid personality disorder. Despite the fact that the majority of the models provided have focused on a single process, it seems that many cognitive, behavioral, and social processes are often involved, which interact and become mutually reinforcing. As a result, rather than being exclusive, competing theories, the mechanisms discussed below (based on research involving participants with a variety of paranoid disorders) should be viewed as descriptions of various possible alternative pathways to paranoia, with their relative importance changing over time.

prejudices in cognition

Paranoid people have an externalizing, personal attributional bias, which means they blame others for unpleasant events in their lives rather than assessing their own possible link to problems (Reference Bentall, Corcoran, and HowardBentall 2001; Reference Bentall and Taylor 2006). Prejudice against others and their perceived malice exacerbates and bends the standard self-serving bias, in which unpleasant outcomes are attributed to external sources (Campbell and SedikidesCampbell 1999). There is a similar tendency to underuse contextual information when explaining negative outcomes (Gilbert, Pelham, and KrullGilbert 1988).

According to Bentall and TaylorBentall (2006), attributional bias is a psychological defense against underlying low self-esteem that is activated when an individual's favorable picture of themselves is challenged. Although there is evidence that individuals with paranoia have low self-esteem in both clinical and non-clinical samples (Martin and Penn, 2001; Ellett, Lopes, and Chadwick, 2003; Combs and Penn, 2004), the relationship between self-esteem, paranoid thinking, and behavior is complex. As previously stated, there is evidence of subgroups with low self-esteem and mood who believe the perceived persecution is justified - 'bad-me paranoia' (Chadwick, Trower, and Juusti-Butler 2005). In such cases, the outward defense of external attribution of responsibility may be only partly effective in suppressing gloomy feelings.

Factors influencing data processing:

Contextual, situational attributions often need more information and cognitive resources than external, personal attributions. When cognitive load increases, people tend to gravitate toward external, personal, 'paranoid' attributions as a default option. This may be related to the proposed link between paranoid illnesses and brain injury (MunroMunro 1988). Hearing loss, for example, has long been associated with an increased risk of paranoid thinking.

Small functional deficiencies affecting social skills have been linked to paranoia. Social anxiety and subclinical paranoia have been linked to emotional and social perception deficits (Combs and PennCombs, 2004). Deficits in 'theory of mind', or the ability to discern the intentions and mental states of others, have also been linked to paranoid thinking.

This may make establishing situational (rather than personal) attributions for negative social interactions more difficult, since inability to understand another person's point of view may encourage personal attributions. For example, failing to see that a colleague may have been distracted by stress (a situational attribution) may reinforce the personal attribution that the colleague is unpleasant.

Attentional bias, a processing bias that has been proven in both clinical populations, causes paranoid persons to notice and remember threat-related information, and hence obsess on it.

Interpersonal relationships

Some cultural influences tend to cause paranoid thinking in 'normal' people. People with paranoid personalities are more likely to exhibit deviant actions and thoughts in these situations. According to a model based on a research of such social repercussions, certain social settings are more likely to be evaluated in a way that causes 'dysphoric self-consciousness,' which leads to hypervigilance and rumination, as well as the activation of paranoid cognitive biases and behaviors. These may exacerbate feelings of insecurity, culminating in a vicious cycle .

The following factors make these cycles more likely:

- feeling dissimilar to the rest of the social group, such as because of gender, skin color, or amount of experience
- attracting the attention of people with more influence, such as senior executives.
- Concerns about one's social status, such as when establishing a new company.

Others have similarly emphasized the possibilities of paranoid thinking in settings involving:

- Unexpected social isolation or loss.
- Significant disruption of normal social networks.
- exposure to contexts where previous social skills may be rendered useless, such as immigration or prison.
- significant sensory deficiencies.
- Genuine weakness and tyranny.

Paranoid personality disorder, by definition, has long-term characteristics that are noticeable even in the absence of such events. Understanding how such events may inspire paranoid thinking, on the other hand, not only aids in predicting when paranoid personality disorder symptoms will develop, but also distinguishes paranoid personality disorder from normal responses to certain situations.

Downward spiral of paranoia

Many of these cognitive, behavioral, and social processes may reinforce one another, resulting in fatal cycles of increasing paranoia. Such pathways may make therapeutic change more difficult to attain.

People with paranoid personality disorder are predisposed to the self-perpetuating processes listed below.

Finding evidence of ill intent in at least some people is usually possible, and this is commonly seen as confirming proof that the individual was 'right all along' to be suspicious.

However, if other individuals seem to be acting innocently, this might be a "front" or "trickery."

Proving a negative, such as that a spouse is not having an affair, is conceptually difficult; the absence of proof may be regarded as confirmation of a "cover-up."

People with paranoid personality disorder are often socially isolated and too cautious while interacting with others. This may discourage people from approaching someone who is ill, leading them to be rude and alienate that individual.

Such conditions may exacerbate a person's anxiety while also increasing their isolation, a self-fulfilling prediction known as "reciprocal determinism" (HaynesHaynes 1986). This cycle may be seen in obstinate, persistent complainers who, in general, provoke more aggressive and negative conduct from people in power (Mullen and LesterMullen 2006).

Because persistent social withdrawal limits social input, a paranoid person's worldview may face unique challenges: it is difficult to learn via experience that others can be trusted if interpersonal relationships do not occur.

As a result, changing paranoid thinking and behavior may be difficult, creating a self-sustaining, self-defeating cycle (Kramer 1998).

The threat of violence

People with paranoid personality disorder are more likely to engage in interpersonal violence because they see others' behaviors as hostile. The majority of research data is derived from paranoid characteristics that typically fall short of a diagnosable paranoid personality disorder and are commonly present in conjunction with other significant risk factors. As a result, although there is evidence that paranoid characteristics increase the likelihood of violence, a person with paranoid personality disorder should not be expected to exhibit such behavior in a high-risk form.

Cross-sectional research has shown that paranoid personality characteristics are associated with histories of both violent, and antisocial behavior. Teenage delinquency has also been linked to paranoid characteristics such as mistreatment, victimization, deception, and being the target of false rumors . A large longitudinal study conducted in the United States discovered that paranoid tendencies in adolescence predicted aggression and criminal behavior in later adolescence and early adulthood, even after accounting for several potential confounding factors.

A meta-analysis of non-clinical populations found that the personality trait of excessive rumination, which is expected in paranoid personality disorder, is associated with a proclivity for aggressive behavior, but only when provoked.

This shows that aggressive behavior in paranoid people requires some provocation. However, due to their various cognitive and perceptual impairments, their threshold for feeling provoked may be exceedingly low; another study found that paranoid symptoms were linked to the commencement of violent disputes. Specific anxieties about intimate relationship faithfulness, which are often associated with paranoid personality disorder, are also linked to an increased risk of threatening and initiating violence against the partner and others.

Pathways to Violence in Paranoia.

People who exhibit paranoid thinking are more likely to behave aggressively for a variety of reasons. Current theories of aggression acknowledge considerable biases in cognitive processing, emotion regulation, and social information processing. Individuals with low self-esteem and sensitivity to social standing may be too sensitive to imagined dangers to status as well as actual safety. As a result, a paranoid individual may be inclined to engage in both punitive and preventive violent behavior against others.

They are also more likely to be suspicious and angry about perceived attacks, ruminating on previous wrongdoings committed by others, which may increase their risk of violence. Furthermore, the previously discussed 'malignant spiral,' in which people with paranoia's suspicious, unusual behavior easily elicits hostility in others, may increase the likelihood that they will encounter actual hostile behavior from others, increasing the likelihood of aggression even more.

Comorbid illnesses are critical in diagnosing and reducing the risk of violence in a paranoid individual. The combination of a paranoid tendency to see others as hostile and low internal barriers to violence (for example, as part of an antisocial personality structure) is particularly distressing (Blackburn & Coid Blackburn 1999). When acute mental illness predominates in paranoid personality disorder, lower inhibitory thresholds for violent behavior due to psychotic, mood, or anxiety symptoms may be applicable (Kennedy, Kemp, and Dyer Kennedy 1992; Buchanan, Reed, and Wessel Buchanan 1993; Taylor 1998; Hodgins, Hiscoke, and Freese Hodgins 2003).

Stalking, issuing threats, and abnormal complaining (Reference Mullen and Lester Mullen 2006) are all negative behaviors associated with paranoid personality traits.

Therapies for paranoid personality disorder
There have been no randomized controlled trials on any of the recommended treatments for paranoid personality disorder. Despite this, the sickness should not be regarded incurable, and there is universal agreement on basic criteria to follow when attempting to adequately handle the issue (Reference Gabbard and GabbardGabbard 2000; Reference FaginFagin 2004).

Fundamental concepts

differential diagnosis and comorbidity

As previously stated, identifying and treating paranoid personality disorder necessitates taking into account any associated personality disorders and/or mental health issues.

Goals of treatment

According to Bernstein et al. (2007), viable long-term treatment goals include:

- embrace and value their own vulnerability.
- improve their self-esteem.
- Improve your reputation with folks.

They express their thoughts openly rather than using negative techniques like shunning or bullying others.

As with many personality disorders, progress is likely to be slow; some estimate that at least 12 months of treatment may be required to determine whether or if therapy is beneficial (Bateman and Tyrer Bateman 2004).

Countertransference

Patients with paranoid personality disorder are more likely to elicit intense protective and even aggressive countertransference responses from their practitioners. Clinicians should avoid reflexive counterattacks, which frequently result in disengagement or violence. They should be wary of minimizing the possibility of violence due to overconfidence or plain denial, particularly with female patients. They should be honest and tough when necessary, and explain why certain decisions were made, even if they were unpopular. Expect to face pushback.

Rejection of authority and sensitivity.

Others are more likely than not to refer people with paranoid symptoms to treatment. Coercive therapy is neither ethical nor legally permissible in the absence of a coexisting mental disorder. People with paranoid personality disorder may participate in meaningful therapy, but using force or deceit is unlikely to achieve results. The physician should avoid raising concerns. For example, if communication happens between several experts involved in the patient's treatment, the patient should be informed. The source of the information in the file (whether from the patient or another source) must be clearly identified. It is critical to assist the patient in maintaining their dignity and feeling as if they have some control over their life and treatment.

Administration of boundaries

Paranoid individuals are more likely to regard a clinician's kind gestures or words of encouragement as a cover for more nefarious intentions. As a result, adopting a 'warm' therapy plan is not recommended. Avoid physical contact and sitting too close together. A paranoid attitude would most certainly need more physical space than the average person. In general, group therapy should be avoided.

Unbalanced emotions.

Any changes in the patient's mood need to be reported to the doctor. Patients may feel genuine anguish (and maybe suicidal ideation) when they realize how their paranoid activities have alienated them. If clinical evidence indicates that a depressive condition is deteriorating, antidepressant medication should be given.

Psychotherapy

Individuals with severe personality disorders, especially those who exhibit paranoid symptoms, may benefit in the long run from a combination of psychosocial residential care and psychotherapy (Chiesa and FonagyChiesa 2003). Individual supportive dynamic psychotherapy (Gabbard and Gabbard, 2000) and schema therapy (Young, Klosko, and Weishaar, 2003) have also been recommended as treatments for PPD.

Beck and colleagues' cognitive therapy approach for paranoid personality disorder (Reference Beck, Freeman, Davis, Beck, Freeman, and DavisBeck 2004) may be the most successful for general psychiatrists. The essential concept is that clinical paranoia is a systematized and too broad representation of a normal adaptive psychological process. Because the underlying cognitive model is one of inadequacy, the primary goal of such therapy is to boost the individual's sense of self-efficacy while openly confessing to being skeptical about therapeutic support, especially in the early stages.

Social abilities such as assertiveness, communication, and empathy may also improve. Longer term, the impulse to assign blame is questioned and addressed in order to disrupt the malignant cycle. Specific goals may include the belief that others are always hostile and dishonest, or that one must always be prepared for danger. The practice of 'collaborative empiricism,' in which the therapist and patient examine the patient's points of view in light of objective evidence, may be effective. Throughout this process, it is important to recognize that the patient's concerns about others may be grounded in reality.

Pharmacotherapy

Medication's role in pure paranoid personality disorder is uncertain. If such diseases are considered to be on a continuum with delusional disorders, antipsychotic treatment may be allowed (Kendler and

Gruenberg, 1982). However, no such medications are now explicitly approved for this use.

Coexisting issues, such as depression and anxiety disorders, as well as the onset of psychotic diseases, may demand therapy.

Skepticism about other people's intentions is common, especially in certain social settings. Such thinking, on the other hand, has the potential to be both harmful and counterproductive. Those with paranoid features may be found in a variety of settings, including formerly healthy persons who have been subjected to significant stress, those suffering from mental illness, and those suffering from personality disorders, most notably paranoid personality disorder. Despite the lack of scientific research on paranoid personality disorder, psychiatrists may diagnose and treat this complex and serious condition by investigating underlying psychological processes and using specific treatment strategies.

Emotional Landscape: Feelings and Reactions in PPD.

What is the male incidence of postpartum depression?

10% to 20% of new mothers suffer from PPD. Although boys are less likely to get PPD, it is not uncommon.

Fathers, unlike birth mothers, are less routinely checked for PPD, which may lead to an increase in men underreporting symptoms.

This makes estimating the number of guys with PPD difficult. PPD, on the other hand, is estimated to affect one in every ten guys.

"PPD is a much more common phenomenon in men than many people believe," says psychotherapist Saqib Bajwa. "Within 3 to 6 months after the birth of a child, 8%-10% of males experience an uncertain range of acute emotions, with depression leading the way.

While there are well-established diagnostic criteria for PPD in women, there are none for men, and it is still unknown how many men suffer from the condition.

"Because this isn't talked about or treated very often, there isn't good evidence on how widespread this is," therapist Marcella Blum says. "Men are often misdiagnosed with other mental health illnesses.

Why do guys have postpartum depression?

Despite recent study, psychologists and psychiatrists remain perplexed about the causes or risk factors for PPD in men. They do feel that a few factors might have a significant impact on PPD in fathers.

Newborns evoke strong emotions.

Even if you did not go through the actual delivery procedure, your environment changed, affecting your sleep, stress, relationships, and other factors.

Renee Goff, a certified clinical psychologist, adds that "[men] may have strong emotions upon seeing what their partner went through to give birth, especially if the delivery was painful or there were complications.

Following the birth of a child, men may lose touch with their spouse as parental instincts take over and the focus shifts to the infant and how to care for the baby, perhaps leading to marital troubles.

"They are experiencing a change in the family dynamic, and often do not feel the strong connection that mothers may feel with their babies, so [they] may feel guilt, shame, or helplessness," Blum says. Some fathers believe that in order to be present in their relationship, they must suppress their emotions.

Insufficient sleep.

"One key element of PPD for males is a lack of sleep," notes Blum. "As we all know, sleep deprivation can cause poor concentration, irritability, melancholy, hunger swings, and weight gain."

She goes on to say that this "may impact a father's capacity to function throughout the early months of fatherhood just as much as it affects a mother's ability to properly bond with motherhood."

Hormonal fluctuations

While hormonal changes in the birthing parent are well established, research suggests that becoming a parent may also have hormonal effects on the non-birthing parent.

According to a 2011 study, testosterone levels in new fathers dropped by 26%-34% (depending on the time of day) after their baby was born. The same study found that males who spent the most time caring for their children had lower testosterone levels as their attachment to their child increased.

Testosterone dips are assumed to be the mechanism by which a man's body suppresses aggression while increasing empathetic responsiveness to a wailing infant. However, as Blum points out, when testosterone levels decline, it may have an effect on

mood, sleep, appetite, and motivation

An early 2007 study also shown that parents may suffer hormonal swings throughout pregnancy and for many months after their child is delivered.

These hormonal abnormalities included a decrease in testosterone and a rise in:

Estrogen, cortisol, vasopressin, and prolactin are all hormones.

While hormone changes may help parents bond with their newborns, they may also increase your risk of PPD.

History of mental disease.

According to Goff, having a history of depression before to having a child may increase your chances of developing PPD. This applies whether you are the mother or father, cisgender or transgender.

Symptoms of PPD differ from one to person, but the most common symptoms, as with women, are concern and sadness.

Men often describe their sensations as follows:

Powerlessness and guilt-based resentment

Other possible symptoms are:

energy spent feeling uncomfortable or concerned, lack of enthusiasm in activities.

Changes in hunger, trouble focusing, aggressive behaviour, and impulsiveness

irritability

The difficulty of adjusting one's weight when sleeping

Suicidal thoughts and feelings of seclusion are difficult. Thoughts of causing harm to the child

Preventing suicide

Remember that you are not alone and that there are options available to you. If you need to talk with someone right now, call the National Suicide Prevention Lifeline at 800-273-8255, which is open 24 hours a day, seven days a week.

The Crisis Textline may be reached by texting "HOME" to 741741.

If you are not in the United States, Befrienders Worldwide may be able to assist you find a hotline in your country.

The Effects of PPD

"Parents usually ignore PPD because of the stigma associated with it," Goff explains. "In today's society, guys are generally expected to 'just get over it,' suck it up,' or 'be a man.' Additionally, a guy who is 'mad and impatient' is more socially acceptable."

Postpartum depression may have a negative impact on your mental health as well as your family and child.

A 2011 study indicated that neonates of sad fathers reported greater levels of discomfort, while another 2011 study discovered that kids of sad fathers may have a higher risk of developing emotional or behavioral issues.

A 2016 study linked parental depression to aggressiveness in children aged 0 to 4, while a 2017 study discovered that father depression increased the likelihood of a kid developing a mental disorder in early childhood.

It may also impact your connection with your spouse, resulting in:

The diagnosis of conflict and separation

Because non-birthing mothers and dads are seldom systematically examined, if you are suffering PPD symptoms, you should see your doctor or therapist.

Your doctor may use a test to rule out any other underlying medical causes for your symptoms.

Treatment

If you've been diagnosed with PPD, your doctor or therapist may assist you in developing a suitable treatment plan. You may need to test a few different things before determining what works best for you.

Treatment regimens for PPD often include a combination of the following:

Therapy, medication support groups, caregiver assistance, self-care, and lifestyle changes are all choices.

The steps are as follows:

Men and non-birthing wives' symptoms of postpartum depression are often overlooked. PPD, on the other hand, may be a devastating disorder for both parents and fathers, wreaking havoc on

Relationships between children's health and wellness

It is not feasible to "muscle through" or "just get over" PPD symptoms. Ignoring PPD symptoms won't help. Getting professional help may be beneficial, despite the stigma and hurdles.

If you believe you may have PPD, know that you are not alone. It is critical to consult with your doctor or therapist if you are experiencing symptoms.

Postpartum depression may be treated in both men and women, frequently using a mix of:

Psychotherapy, medicine, self-care, and lifestyle modifications.

Social assistance

If you're looking for assistance, websites like PostpartumDepression.org may be an excellent place to begin. You should also read Psych Central's advice for getting mental health treatment.

Chapter 6

Here are some suggestions for coping with a paranoid spouse.

What is the actual meaning of paranoia?

Before we go into how to cope with paranoid thinking, let's define it.

Paranoid is a term often used to describe someone who is suspicious, repressed, mistrustful, or feels they are being exploited. But it goes beyond that. These qualities indicate that the person has low self-esteem, is pessimistic, or has had adverse occurrences that have shaped their view.

People who are paranoid have difficulties trusting people.

As a consequence, individuals often struggle to build close social and personal relationships. Delusional disorder, paranoid personality disorder, and schizophrenia are all possible causes of paranoia. Let's look at what they represent.

Delusional condition.

This condition leads individuals to create delusory beliefs. They will not show any signs of mental illness, but will believe in something that does not exist in reality. People may believe they are a Crowned Prince or have a link with a renowned celebrity they have never met.

Paranoia is a kind of personality disorder.

This is the mildest kind of paranoia. Individuals suffering from this will have difficulty trusting others or the world. This is something that people develop as a consequence of severe life experiences.

Schizophrenia with paranoid symptoms.

This is the most severe kind of paranoia, in which the person has weird and ludicrous delusions. Individuals, for example, may assume that their thoughts or personal lives are being broadcast globally via social media. People have hallucinations as well.

Now that we've determined the most common paranoid condition, let's talk about how to deal with paranoid people.

Managing a paranoid coworker.

What are the causes of paranoid personality disorder?

Although the specific etiology of paranoid personality disorder is uncertain, the following are some possible causes of paranoia.

1. Biological components.

According to studies, our DNA influences some of our personality characteristics. According to several studies, genetics may have a role in the development of paranoid personality disorder.

According to the aforementioned studies, paranoid personality disorder is widespread in families with a history of psychosis.

It is unclear if such illogical behavior is passed down genetically to future generations, although it is quite plausible.

2. Brain injury.

Research indicates a link between brain injury and the development of a paranoid personality disorder. Some people develop paranoia following a brain injury.

3. Additional factors.

While genetics play a major role, a person's environment may have a considerable impact on the development of a paranoid personality disorder. Childhood trauma, parental neglect, bullying, or molestation may all have a severe impact on mental health and could lead to paranoid personality disorder.

What are the implications of paranoid personality disorder for relationships?

It is tough to love someone with paranoid personality disorder. It has its own set of challenges, and in order to maintain the connection, you must learn how to deal with a misguided person. Here are a few examples of how paranoia impacts relationships.

The paranoid person may have difficulty trusting their partner and may seek unnecessary confirmation of their whereabouts from anybody.

A paranoid person may be extremely critical and unpleasant toward their partner.

Because of their lack of sensitivity, they may inadvertently damage their spouse's feelings and then blame them.

They may remember every detail of your conduct and carry anger against you.

They may have a negative attitude about their partner and the relationship. They may engage in passive-aggressive behavior against their partner.

They may want ultimate control over their relationships and life. They may order you to discontinue all communication with friends and family.

5 ways for coping with a paranoid spouse.

If you live with someone who has just been diagnosed with paranoia, know that the path ahead will be difficult. There may be moments when you want to abandon everything, but you will be unable to do so since others depend on you.

In such grave circumstances, your patience will be tested frequently. So, how do you handle someone who suffers from paranoia? Here are five techniques for coping with a paranoid spouse.

1. Encourage and support them in their drug-related activities.

Once you've demonstrated that your partner has paranoia, you need to know how to cope with someone who is paranoid.

Please encourage them to get medical care to better their life. It may be difficult for them to trust doctors and refuse medications, but you must convince them for their own good.

Consistently provide support and assistance. Early identification and treatment of this condition may simplify and enhance quality of life.

2. Set clear boundaries within your relationship.

This condition is characterized by mistrust, distrust, and persistent suspicion.

This may create mental discomfort, and you may often find yourself on the edge of breaking up with your sweetheart.

To avoid such debates, it is necessary to set limitations. This is how paranoid claims are handled.

Consult an expert and discuss your options with them. This will keep your boyfriend from abusing you out of paranoia.

3. Develop your communication abilities.

You may not realize it, yet we make inaccurate or unclear comments every day.

We discover out when we start living with a paranoid person. As a consequence, in order to avoid disagreements or arousing their paranoia, you must develop the practice of communicating honestly and in unambiguous language.

This may help you retain a solid bond with your partner while keeping their issue from harming you.

Watch this video to discover how to improve your communication skills.

4. Determine likely reasons.

If you want to know how to deal with a delusional or paranoid spouse, you must first understand why they are behaving this way. Keep a watch out for circumstances that worsen their symptoms and avoid them.

Instead, accentuate their positive qualities and skills. You should examine the chance that they do not understand how to deal with paranoia.

5. Start stressing excellent social relationships and self-care.

Self-care is crucial for everyone, yet we sometimes take it for granted. If you live with a paranoid person, now is the time to pay attention. Begin with self-care and encourage your partner to do the same. This enables you to surround yourself with positive energy, which helps you both feel better.

Similarly, paranoid people want to isolate themselves from their surroundings because they believe others are untrustworthy. This may be avoided if you both take little steps toward a healthy social life.

Spend lots of time with your family and closest friends. Make your spouse feel supported by highlighting the presence of caring individuals in their life.

Takeaway

The uncertainty of the future keeps us in the dark about what is ahead. Unexpected changes might occur, causing confusion and pushing us to choose between ignoring or tackling the difficulties. However, abandoning is not an option in the context of relationships, particularly with a paranoid spouse. Addressing the issue becomes vital. Following suggestions on coping with a paranoid spouse may help your condition.

Please watch the Nigerian film MARRIED TO THE DEVIL to have a better understanding of the devastation PPD can do to relationships.

For more information on paranoid causes, signs, symptoms, and treatments, please refer to my other book, Paranoid Personality Disorder: The Ultimate Guide for Spouses on How to Understand Symptoms, Treatment, and Prevention of PPD.

Chapter 7

10 Simple Steps to Reduce Paranoia in Your Relationship

Your poisonous relationship behaviour has resurfaced.

You are growing uncomfortable, distrustful of your partner, and paranoid.

You're wondering whether they are really madly in love with you.

You begin to interpret their actions as signs that they are about to leave you - a text that they did not react to right away, an evening when you thought something was "off" with them, a nagging suspicion — baseless but there — that he is seeing another woman.

Do you have experience with relationship anxiety and paranoia? Do you identify the pattern?

If this is the case, you should be aware that you may be eligible for aid.

Let's discuss how to get rid of mistrust in a relationship.

Relationships and anxiety are intricately intertwined.

Sometimes these two things work well together.

Most people, on the other hand, deal with anxiety by positive self-talk, good communication methods, and seeking professional help if they think it is necessary.

Some of us, on the other hand, endure severe anxiety in both personal and professional interactions.

Why do some people manage their paranoia and anxiety, while others remain trapped in a vicious cycle?

Relationship paranoia causes

What's the source of your relationship paranoia? Once you've identified the causes and effects of relationship paranoia, it will be easier to understand how to stop being suspicious in a relationship. To understand more about paranoid causes, symptoms, signs, and treatments, click here to get a comprehensive guidebook.

1. Your previous experiences may impact your future choices.

So much of your background will influence your conduct in the future.

Assume you had trauma in a previous relationship or as a child and have yet to complete the arduous but necessary psychological work needed to heal yourself. In this case, you would very probably carry this into future relationships.

If trust issues are not addressed honestly, they are very difficult to resolve.

Assume your previous lover was disloyal to you. Assume he maintained his extramarital affairs covert for several years until they were disclosed.

Because you spent years with someone you thought was trustworthy but turned out to be living a double life, it's normal to have trust issues in future relationships.

2. problems with self-esteem

You are more likely to be paranoid in your relationship if you have low self-esteem. You may feel that your spouse is too good for you or that they can always find a better match. In such a scenario, you would be constantly apprehensive about their leaving.

3. Attachment Fashions

People develop different attachment styles as a consequence of their formative experiences. Some people have an anxious attachment style, which breeds suspicion and concern even in mature love relationships.

What are the next steps?

Effects of Relationship Paranoia

Relationship paranoia may jeopardize your health, partner, and relationships. Understanding the implications of relationship paranoia may help you decide how to stop being suspicious in your relationship.

1. Maintaining one's health

Paranoia causes your brain to become hypervigilant. As a consequence, you may have increased stress, sleep deprivation, reduced appetite, worry, and fatigue.

2. Your partner is having problems coping with it.

While your partner may comprehend your point of view, constantly worrying about them or your relationship may be bad to them. They may feel compelled to defend themselves at all times, which is both detrimental and difficult for them.

3. The connection lacks trust.

Relationship paranoia is defined as a lack of confidence in a relationship. Trust is one of the building blocks of a successful relationship, and its lack may harm your connection.

10 suggestions for coping with paranoia in a relationship.
This article will help you learn about practical ways to manage paranoia in your relationship. If you've ever wondered, "How can I address paranoia in my relationship?" this guide is for you.

1. Have a free and open debate.
How do you cope with paranoia throughout a relationship?
If you are concerned about trust in your current relationship, the first thing you should do is talk to your partner.
You must establish if you are being paranoid as a result of a previous relationship experience or whether anything is wrong.
So sit down with your husband and have an open chat.
Tell him how you feel: that you are having paranoia and want to know whether it is genuine.

2. Resolving Old Problems
Ideally, your open chat with your spouse will indicate that there is no need to be suspicious; this is the basis for the answer to the issue "How to stop being paranoid in a relationship?"
However, this may not be sufficient to alleviate your anxiety—remember that trust issues, paranoia, and feelings of uneasiness in a relationship are all indications of long-term emotional baggage.
If you want to have healthy, happy relationships, you must concentrate on altering that response.

3. Recognize your feelings.
Recognize that one of your default sensations is insecurity, which is

about you rather than the connection.

Recognizing this component of your personality is the first step toward overcoming trust issues and paranoia.

This awareness enables you to distinguish negative feelings that emerge from inside rather than elsewhere.

4. Seek professional help.

Trained therapists can assist you in determining the underlying reasons of these behaviors and restoring trust issues in a relationship.

Working with a mental health professional in a safe and trusting atmosphere may help you overcome these relationship-damaging tendencies.

You might learn to replace your paranoia, insecurity, and lack of trust with more positive and loving ideas, which you can repeat until you feel more at ease and capable of letting go of the negative feelings.

5. Pay attention to the present time.

If you want to learn how to stop being suspicious in a relationship, stay focused on the present moment and avoid looking back

It is possible to retrain our brains such that when a negative thought arises, we become aware of how we feel for a little period of time before learning to let it go.

To deal with relationship uncertainty, avoid recalling any previous terrible relationships that have nothing to do with your current living situation.

Each new and intriguing link in your life is a distinct thing.

6. Practice self-care to stop being paranoid.

To overcome your paranoia, practice self-care.

The answer to "How to Not Be Paranoid in a Relationship" is to boost your self-esteem since a low sense of self-worth leads to paranoia, insecurity, and trust issues.

When we have low self-esteem, we may believe that we are unworthy of wonderful things in life or of being in a relationship with our partner.

Our trust issues begin to take a toll on relationships, and the very thing we feared—abandonment—occurs as a result of our actions.

You may prevent becoming suspicious and uneasy in your relationship by taking the effort to create your sense of worth, value, and self-esteem.

Being in a relationship where you know your worth is liberating!

7. Determine your triggers.

Understanding the root of your relationship paranoia is key to defeating it. Is it when you have no clue what your spouse is doing or when you see them hiding their phone from you? Recognizing and avoiding your triggers will help you avoid being paranoid in your relationships.

8. Take a deep breath in before answering.

Your first reactions to anything that triggers your paranoia may be anxiety and confusion; but, take the time to determine what is causing this sensation. Is this the case, or do you have general relationship paranoia.

This may really help you reduce your paranoia.

9. Do not get paranoid.

Resist the impulse to become paranoid when you have these thoughts; understand and manage your emotions, but don't let them control your actions.

10. Focus on developing trust.

Learn how to acquire your partner's trust; exercise and relationship therapy may help you strengthen it.

Trust is crucial.

How can I overcome my paranoia and lack of faith?

Without a doubt, trust is one of the most important aspects of any relationship. Being paranoid in a relationship indicates a lack of trust, which you and your partner must address and work on.

If you believe you need professional assistance, consult with a counselor.

9 Relationship Coping Strategies for Paranoid Schizophrenia.

Paranoid schizophrenia is a kind of schizophrenia that affects a person's thoughts, feelings, and behavior. People with paranoid schizophrenia often fail to distinguish between what is genuine and what is not, which leads to mistaken beliefs or delusions.

Understanding what paranoid schizophrenia is and how to cope with it in relationships is critical, since they may have unwarranted worries or believe that others are attempting to harm them. This may make daily life difficult and create issues in relationships and at work.

Meaning of paranoid schizophrenia:

A paranoid schizophrenic is a person who has a subtype of schizophrenia, a chronic mental disease that is characterized by hallucinations and delusions, which often include a continuous sensation of persecution or grandiosity.

These patients may hear voices or believe that others are scheming against them, causing substantial anguish and compromising everyday functioning. The specific etiology is unknown, although it is likely to be a mix of genetic, neurological, and environmental factors.

How do paranoid schizophrenia and schizophrenia differ?

The primary distinctions between paranoid schizophrenia and schizophrenia in general are as follows:

Focus

Schizophrenia is a wide category with many subcategories, including paranoid, disorganized, catatonic, undifferentiated, and residual.

Symptoms

Schizophrenia, on the other hand, may have a broader range of symptoms such as slurred speech, catatonia, affective flatness, and negative symptoms (such as limited emotional expressiveness), whereas paranoid schizophrenia is distinguished by delusions (usually of persecution or grandiosity) and auditory hallucinations.

There are delusions and hallucinations.

Paranoid schizophrenia is characterized by greater and more frequent delusions and hallucinations, while other symptoms, such as disorganization or emotional unresponsiveness, may be more obvious.

Functional limits.

Individuals with paranoid schizophrenia may have better cognitive functioning and daily living skills than those with other types of schizophrenia; however, other schizophrenia subtypes frequently exhibit more severe abnormalities in cognitive processes, emotional reactivity, and daily functioning.

What factors are included in paranoid schizophrenia?

The young wife begs for forgiveness.

Paranoid schizophrenia, a complicated mental health illness, is caused by a variety of circumstances, including:

A family history of schizophrenia suggests a genetic component.

Neurotransmitter imbalances such as dopamine, as well as anatomical and functional abnormalities in the brain.

Complications during pregnancy or delivery, prenatal malnutrition, and exposure to poisons or viruses are all possible.

Stressful life events, trauma, and social isolation may all trigger or exacerbate symptoms.

Substance misuse, particularly throughout youth, increases the risk of developing the illness.

There are eleven signs of paranoid schizophrenia.

Paranoid schizophrenia is a complex mental disorder characterized by a variety of symptoms that can have a significant impact on a person's life. Understanding these warning signs is critical for early detection and treatment. Here are some of the most common symptoms of paranoid schizophrenia.

1. Delusions.

Delusions are common symptoms of paranoid schizophrenia, a condition in which the individual has strong beliefs that are not supported by reality. These beliefs often include feelings of being persecuted or plotted against, as well as the idea that they have exceptional abilities or reputations. Despite clear evidence to the contrary, these illusions persist.

2. hallucinations

Hallucinations, especially auditory hallucinations, are prevalent in paranoid schizophrenia. People may hear voices that aren't there, which may be disturbing or demanding. These voices may comment on the person's conduct, criticize them, or tell them what to do.

3. That is disorderly thinking.

Disorganized thinking is a significant symptom, making it difficult to arrange ideas rationally. This may result in a difficult-to-follow speech in which the speaker jumps from one topic to the next without making logical links.

4. Emotional withdrawal.

Individuals with paranoid schizophrenia often become emotionally distant from others, which might be due to panic caused by their delusions or a direct outcome of the disorder, such as difficulty expressing emotions.

5. Uncertainty and hostility

Falsely accusing friends or family members of disloyalty or violence may be harmful to relationships, and persecution delusions are often associated with increasing mistrust and enmity.

6. Anxiety and agitation.

Anxiety and agitation are common symptoms, and individuals may experience increased anxiety and restlessness due to the persistent dread and mistrust caused by delusions and hallucinations.

7. lack of insight

Many people with paranoid schizophrenia may not realize that their delusions or hallucinations are symptoms of a mental disease, which complicates treatment.

8. Cognitive problems.

Cognitive impairments, such as difficulty concentrating, remembering, and making choices, are often associated with schizophrenia's paranoid origins. These challenges may have an influence on everyday functioning as well as the capacity to retain a career or relationships.

9. Social isolation.

Fear, distrust, and difficulty talking and connecting with people all contribute to broad social disengagement, which may lead to isolation and worsen other symptoms.

10. Challenges with functioning

The mix of symptoms often causes difficulties in everyday functioning, such as maintaining personal connections, finding work, and managing one's own care.

11. Disorganized conduct is seen.

Disorganized behavior may manifest in a variety of ways, ranging from poor personal cleanliness to erratic and unpredictable conduct, which might be caused by cognitive issues or the illness itself.

How can you cope with paranoid schizophrenia in a relationship? Nine approaches.

A forlorn couple looking for assistance.

Dealing with paranoid schizophrenia in a relationship may be difficult, but with the appropriate attitude and knowledge, you can create a healthy and supportive connection. Here are nine techniques to dealing with someone suffering from paranoid schizophrenia.

1. Learn as much as you can about the disease.

Understanding the symptoms of paranoid schizophrenia, as well as the realities of living with the condition, is essential. The National Institute of Mental Health (NIMH) offers a wealth of resources that may be useful.

2. Show patience and understanding.

Individuals suffering with paranoid schizophrenia may feel tremendous fear and disorientation, so being patient and empathic while they are experiencing symptoms may assist to establish a supportive atmosphere.

3. Encourage the usage of expert services.

It is vital to urge your partner to seek and maintain professional assistance. Medication and therapy may frequently help with the diagnosis of paranoid schizophrenia. urge your spouse to adhere to their treatment plan and attend appointments.

4. Communicate freely and honestly.

Open and honest communication is essential; discuss your worries and urge your partner to do the same in order to better understand and cooperate.

5. Set sensible objectives.

It is crucial to remember that managing paranoid schizophrenia is a continual process. Setting reasonable expectations about the relationship and treatment of paranoid schizophrenia will assist to minimize disappointments and frustrations.

6. Establish the ground rules.

To maintain a good relationship and personal well-being, it's important to discuss and agree on what is and isn't suitable conduct. Then, make sure that these boundaries are respected.

7. Prioritize self-care.

It is also vital to care after your own mental and emotional well-being. Take part in activities that you like and seek support for yourself when required. Remember that if you are not feeling well, you cannot completely assist others.

8. Take use of a support network.

Both spouses may benefit from having a support network. Friends, family, and support groups may all give extra aid and understanding. This network may also provide you with a break, preventing you from being overwhelmed.

Dr. Benzio, a board-certified psychiatrist, provides advise on how to care for and comfort a spouse suffering from mental illness, as well as what to avoid.

9. Be prepared for problems.

Recognize that there may be obstacles. The symptoms of paranoid schizophrenia may surprise you, so prepare for challenging circumstances and have a strategy in place to cope with them. This can involve having emergency contact information or knowing when to seek more help.

FAQs

People who have a loved one with paranoid schizophrenia often have a lot of questions. Here are some of the most often asked questions concerning paranoid schizophrenia, along with short and succinct solutions.

Is paranoid schizophrenia passed down via families?

Although having a family member with schizophrenia raises the risk, it is not necessarily inherited.

Individual experiences and environmental circumstances are also crucial; a genetic predisposition enhances the potential, but not the likelihood, of acquiring the disease.

Is it possible for someone with paranoid schizophrenia to have a normal life?

Yes, individuals with paranoid schizophrenia may live a normal life, particularly with proper medicine and care. Common treatments include medication, therapy, and social support. The importance of early diagnosis and treatment adherence cannot be overemphasized.

Many people with paranoid schizophrenia work, have relationships, and participate in their communities. However, the phrase "normal" might mean various things to different people, and the disease may need frequent modifications and coping strategies.

Is it possible to completely treat paranoid schizophrenia?

Currently, there is no cure for paranoid schizophrenia, but treatment may help control symptoms, prevent relapses, and improve quality of life. The foundations of treatment include medication, particularly antipsychotics, and psychotherapy.

Individuals may have fulfilling lives with competent care, although they may continue to experience specific symptoms or need ongoing therapy.

When does paranoid schizophrenia manifest itself?

Paranoid schizophrenia often appears in late adolescence or early adulthood between the ages of 18 and 30, however it is rare in youngsters and beyond 45 years of age.

Early diagnosis and treatment may lead to a better long-term prognosis, even if changes in cognition, emotion, and behavior are mild warning signs.

What exactly causes paranoid schizophrenia?

Stressful life events, drug abuse, and traumatic experiences may all serve as triggers for paranoid schizophrenia, which can be caused by a mix of genetic, neurological, and environmental factors, particularly in genetically predisposed individuals.

Neurobiological factors, including as chemical imbalances in the brain, also have a role, although it's important to note that the specific triggers might vary greatly across people.

In conclusion.

While maintaining a connection with someone suffering from paranoid schizophrenia might be difficult, the following methods may help to create a supportive and loving environment. Keep in mind that the issue, "Does schizophrenia disappear?" Managing schizophrenia is difficult owing to its lifelong nature; but, with adequate care and support, people may live productive lives.

Consider visiting reputable websites such as the Schizophrenia & Psychosis Action Alliance (S&PAA) for further information and advice on how to help a paranoid schizophrenic.

Chapter 8

The Effects of PPD on Marriage: Coping Strategies for Living with a Paranoid Spouse.

Living with someone who is paranoid needs patience, compassion, and strict personal limits. The tips below may help you provide the necessary support and assistance to help him overcome his paranoia.

Encourage treatment adherence - Due to his suspicious temperament, he may find it difficult to take recommended medications or attend therapy sessions. This is characteristic among people being treated for paranoia, and it greatly hinders their recovery. Encourage him to follow through on his treatment plan.

Shorter sentences and clearer language reduce the possibility of being misread.

Acceptance while being strong is critical since delusions are extremely real for the individual experiencing them. Do not question the individual's viewpoints or attempt to assist him with reality testing. Demonstrate respect for his opinions without seeming to share them.

Be frank about your personal opinions.

Offer an explanation - You may help him overcome his suspicion and mistrust by asking him to voice his ideas and then explaining your actions in a non-defensive and objective manner.

Anticipate triggers: In unfamiliar or stressful situations, symptoms may intensify. Provide relevant information ahead of time so that the person is better prepared for changes and the possibility that symptoms could increase.

Highlight his strengths: Aside from interpersonal interactions, people with paranoia are often brilliant and high-functioning. Pay attention to him as a person, not simply his symptoms. Pay attention to his favorable traits and actions.

Take Care of Yourself.

Caring for an excessively worried spouse may be difficult. To meet his expectations, first address your own. To avoid being overwhelmed, follow the guidelines below.

Strive for balance by giving equal attention to the other aspects of life. Have non-disease-related conversations with him. Engage in activities unrelated to his illness. Keep in mind that his paranoia is just one of your issues, not the primary one.

Maintain your health: Being sick will make it more difficult for you to care for and interact with him. Eat properly, exercise often, and get enough of rest. It will give you more energy, improve your mood, and help you deal with the extra stress.

Educate yourself: learn all you can about his kind of paranoia. Make an attempt to comprehend both the symptoms you see and the treatment he is receiving.

Consult his doctor for clarification and other information.

Consider getting therapy to help you accept his diagnosis and develop coping strategies. Seek encouragement and support from family and friends. Find a support group for the family of a paranoid person.

Consider these resources.

Martin Kantor's Understanding Paranoia: A Guide for Professionals, Families, and Sufferers is a good place to start.

Coping with a loved one's paranoia is difficult, and rehabilitation requires skilled assistance. Seek support for both him and yourself. Learn all you can to better prepare for the next challenges. Above all, understand that you are not alone and that a better future is possible.

Always consult your doctor first.

Although reading and speaking with friends may provide useful health information, you should always see your doctor before beginning a new treatment or changing your diet. Keep in mind that the United States Food and Drug Administration does not strictly regulate the strength, purity, or safety of herbs and supplements. Always read product labels. If you have a medical problem or are on other drugs, herbs, or supplements, see your doctor before changing your health regimen or taking any medical action. This content is not intended to substitute medical advice. LifeScript assumes no responsibility for any actions made by readers based on the information provided.

How to Handle a Relationship With Paranoid Personality Disorder.

You have a lovely, caring, and clever companion who often questions your motives and dedication. You wonder whether they will ever believe you. Understanding if your problems are caused by paranoid personality disorder is a critical step towards healing.

Trust is a key component of successful partnerships because it enhances partners' shared sense of commitment and camaraderie. When trust is lacking, the repercussions for a long-term relationship may be substantial, even disastrous.

People with paranoid personality disorder struggle to trust others, even those they love and deserve to trust, due to a heightened fear of betrayal. They may accuse loved ones of lying, having an affair, spreading rumors about them, or stealing funds. This kind of behavior may be painful and annoying for people who have been falsely accused, as well as disturbing and alienating for others who see it.

Identifying the symptoms of paranoid personality disorder and learning more about how to deal with it, as well as treatment options, may help improve an otherwise strained relationship.

What is the impact of paranoid personality disorder on relationships?

PPD may have serious effects in a relationship, perhaps leading to its breakup, since it is largely concerned with trust issues, and trust is a necessary component of every good relationship. This is exacerbated by the fact that the great majority of PPD patients are uninformed of their diagnosis and are unable to see how their viewpoint might be harmful.

The following are the most common PPD-related worries that adversely impact a relationship:

Pessimism: People with PPD see the worst in others. It's not that they can't see the good; it's just that they believe there's always the risk of something going wrong. This may lead a partner to feel that no matter what they do, they will never be able to establish a trustworthy or loyal relationship.

Suspicion - Because the fear of betrayal prevents trust, even the most innocent activities are tainted. Partners who feel their significant other is hiding anything may struggle to explain everyday occurrences such as a missed call from the wrong number or a change in plans due to traffic.

Stubbornness - While someone with PPD may sometimes concede that they were wrong in a given situation, they are more prone to refuse to let go of attitudes or beliefs about others, even when evidence says otherwise, resulting in unresolved confrontations or disagreements. This might lead to long-held grudges and falling outs with once close friends.

Controlling conduct - A person suffering from PPD may attempt to cope with their anxiety by keeping a watch on others around them. This might include making several phone calls to check on their partner's location, joining them on outings or parties, and often seeking reassurance.

Criticism - Because people with PPD are unable to see errors in their own viewpoints, they often blame others for defects or blunders. When they are insulted, they may become judgmental or angry. This is especially bad when the other side has done nothing wrong.

When such difficulties continue in a relationship, both sides may feel stressed, depressed, and worried. When a spouse avoids people because of paranoid ideas and attempts to further control the couple's environment, it may be alienating. Seeking professional assistance in this situation is critical for establishing trust, boosting communication, and creating a healthy relationship.

Managing the Paranoid Personality Disorder.

If not addressed, paranoid personality disorder may cause unnecessary injury or even the loss of otherwise good and valuable relationships. Learning how to deal with paranoid personality disorder may improve a relationship's long-term outcomes as well as both partners' overall pleasure.

If you are in a relationship with someone who you feel has PPD, you may do a few things to help reduce the effects.

Create clear limits - While being supportive and empathetic to your relationship is important, you should also set clear boundaries to protect yourself and your needs, as well as limit how far you will go in response to a partner's reaction or allegation.

Do not dispute or engage - Because people with PPD are usually adamant in their situational judgments, arguing or even attempting to comfort them will not change their views. Empathizing with the individual's feelings while disagreeing or agreeing with the facts may help to support the person while avoiding views based on fear rather than reality.

Maintain your social networks - People with PPD may feel lonely, especially if their accusations and suspicions of others drive more people away or prevent them from connecting with a large number of friends, family, and coworkers. Maintaining supportive relationships with others is essential for breaking the cycle of isolation, which may impair both you and your partner's mental health.

Consider seeking professional help; your partner may be resistant to treatment at first, and forcing them to attend therapy may exacerbate their PPD symptoms. Reaching out to a professional on your own, on the other hand, may be advantageous in terms of providing a competent support system while working on your relationship, as well as an outlet for your own thoughts, concerns, or frustrations.

How To Survive A Paranoid Partner's Relationship

If your partner suffers from paranoia, it may arise and wane over the relationship, but it will typically be there. Paranoia is usually manifested as a desire for total control. In romantic relationships, control seeking may take many forms, including information gathering, interrogation, searching, reorganizing, spying, monitoring, false charges, trap laying, and hacking into another person's phone and computer.

Typically, all of these characteristics are present.

The paranoid person may not consider these activities uncommon, and may even try to convince you that they are normal in a relationship. Don't be misled by this line of thinking. These are anxiety-reduction strategies that come at the expense of others.

Nobody can really know everything about another person, so why would you want to? Do you really need to know every bodily function in your relationship, or that they think your mother is a b-word, or that a waiter destroyed a plate over lunch? Clearly not.

That is why, depending on each individual's circumstances, we adapt and/or share.

Many paranoid people worry about little things. Consider a possible slight or falsehood. Facts are not facts when exploited by paranoid people.

Paranoia has a significant psychological and physical influence on both parties in the relationship. If you want to stay in a paranoid love relationship, here are seven things to do.

The first step in resolving paranoia with a spouse is to convey your wish for a healthy relationship. One of the least terrifying methods to face your spouse about the issue is to communicate your ideas, the acts that have interrupted the connection, and your desire for the relationship to function and flourish. This may need to be repeated: allegations and constant monitoring contributed to your mental health degradation. Never, ever quit up.

Seek expert help. Couples therapy may be especially helpful for couples who want to lessen the effects of paranoia in their relationship. Keep your treatment request succinct and to the point. Because of the high levels of distrust associated with paranoia, the first treatment sessions may be difficult. The paranoid person is likely to be dubious of the whole treatment strategy. It is vital to spend time getting to know the therapist and letting your partner talk at their own pace. Continue to embrace your feelings and reactions to your partner's paranoid behavior, and remember to be true to yourself.

When your partner is paranoid, their viewpoint is distorted.

You should never admit or accept blame for bogus accusations, since this will just intensify your paranoia. I worked with a couple in which the husband admitted to kissing another woman despite the wife's constant and severe questions about his loyalty. He said that he just wanted the questioning to stop and thought that this was the best way to help them move on. Unfortunately, this heightened the wife's suspicions, and she filed for divorce from her faithful husband.

Remember to take care of yourself. Yoga, exercise, meditation, deep breathing, and a well-balanced diet may all help you reduce emotional stress and improve your mental clarity.

If you get melancholy or frightened, you may need psychiatric treatment.

Seek assistance from a trustworthy someone, such as a friend, family member, or therapist. Having a nonjudgmental voice recognize your feelings may be calming and grounding while you work on your relationship. When people in paranoid relationships admit the truth about their relationship, they often feel lonely and ashamed. Unfortunately, this just exacerbates the loneliness and worry.

Consider taking a break from your relationship to cleanse your mind. This may be accomplished by either moving out or putting the relationship on hold temporarily. While this may be daunting for the paranoid, some distance is required to verify that your thoughts are fair and beneficial to both parties. Making time for oneself is crucial.

Paranoia may manifest as depression, PTSD, psychosis, paranoid personality disorder, schizophrenia, or schizoaffective disorder. Do not try to diagnose your companion on your own. Seek help from a mental health professional to assess his or her individual issues and, more significantly, to restore your own peace of mind.

If you no longer feel like yourself, know that you may regain your previous self. Do not succumb to paranoia.

III

Part Three

Professional Guidance, Trust Issues, and Real-Life Success Stories in Overcoming PPD

This section provides valuable insights into seeking professional help, understanding and addressing trust issues in relationships, and real-life accounts of individuals who have successfully navigated postpartum depression. Through expert advice and personal stories, we aim to offer practical support and hope for those affected by PPD.

Chapter 9

Seeking Professional Help: The Value of Diagnosis

To establish if you have postpartum baby blues or a more severe kind of depression, your doctor will often ask you about your emotions, thoughts, and mental health. Do not feel embarrassed if you suffer from postpartum depression. Inform your doctor about your symptoms so that you and your doctor can devise an appropriate treatment strategy.

As part of your examination, your healthcare practitioner may do a depression screening, which may involve asking you to complete a questionnaire. Your physician may prescribe further tests to rule out other potential reasons of your symptoms.

Treatment

Treatment and recovery timelines vary according to the severity of your depression and your specific demands. If you have an underactive thyroid or another underlying disease, your doctor may recommend that you see a specialist. Your doctor may also recommend you to a mental health provider.

The newborn blues

The baby blues usually fade away after a few days or a week. For the time being.

- Get enough sleep.
- Accept help from family and friends.
- Connect with other new mothers.
- Set aside time to seek for yourself.

Avoid using alcohol and recreational drugs, since they might exacerbate mood fluctuations.

If you're having trouble producing milk or breastfeeding, speak with your doctor about hiring a lactation consultant.

Depression After Childbirth

Psychotherapy, often known as talk therapy or mental health counseling, drugs, or a combination of the two, are commonly used to treat postpartum depression.

Psychotherapy. It may be beneficial to discuss your concerns with a psychiatrist, psychologist, or another mental health expert. Therapy may help you discover better ways to manage your emotions, solve issues, create realistic objectives, and react to situations in a healthy way. Counseling for families and relationships may also be beneficial. Postpartum depression is treated with cognitive-behavioral therapy (CBT) and interpersonal psychotherapy.

Antidepressants. Your doctor may suggest that you take an antidepressant. If you are breastfeeding, any medications you take will pass into your breast milk. Most antidepressants, on the other hand, may be taken during nursing with little danger to your kid. Discuss the risks and advantages of different antidepressants with your doctor.

Other medications. If required, further drugs may be added to your regimen. For example, if you have postpartum depression along with significant anxiety or sleeplessness, you may be prescribed an antianxiety medication for a brief period of time.

Brexanolone (Zulresso) is the first medication licensed by the US Food and Drug Administration for adult women experiencing postpartum depression. Brexanolone decreases the fast drop of some hormones after delivery, which may contribute to postpartum depression. Because of the risk of major adverse effects, the medication must be injected via a vein and monitored by a healthcare professional for 60 hours. As a consequence, the therapy is not generally accessible right now.

The development of an oral medication for postpartum depression is still underway, and the results are encouraging. The drug under research operates in the same manner as brexanolone. However, if taken on a regular basis as a tablet, it may not have the same negative side effects.

Symptoms of postpartum depression often improve with adequate treatment. In rare situations, postpartum depression may progress to persistent depression. It is critical to maintain therapy after you are feeling better. If you stop therapy too soon, you may have a recurrence.

Psychosis after delivery.
Postpartum psychosis need rapid medical care, often in a hospital. Among the therapy alternatives are:
Medicines. To moderate your symptoms, you may need to take a combination of drugs, such as antidepressants, antipsychotics, mood stabilizers, or benzodiazepines.

Electroconvulsive therapy is shortened as ECT. If medication fails to alleviate your symptoms of postpartum depression and psychosis, ECT may be considered. ECT is a process in which tiny electrical currents are purposely sent to the brain, causing a short seizure. ECT seems to alter brain chemistry, which may alleviate symptoms of psychosis and depression, particularly when other therapies have failed.

A hospital stay for postpartum psychosis treatment might make nursing difficult. Breastfeeding becomes difficult since the baby is separated. While you're in the hospital, your doctor may assist you with lactation (the production of breast milk).

Home remedies and lifestyle

In addition to expert treatment, there are various things you may do on your own to speed up your recovery.

Choose a healthy way of living. Include physical activity in your regular routine, such as taking a walk with your infant or engaging in other types of exercise. Make an effort to obtain enough sleep. Avoid drinking and eat nourishing meals.

Set appropriate expectations. Avoid putting yourself under too much stress. Reduce your aspirations for the perfect family. Do your best, and leave the rest to others.

Make time for yourself. Get out of the home and get some alone time. This may involve seeking the assistance of a spouse or hiring a sitter. Participate in an activity or kind of entertainment that you like. You might also plan some alone time with your spouse or buddies.

Isolation should be avoided at all cost. Share your feelings with your spouse, family, and friends. Inquire about other mother's experiences. Breaking your seclusion may allow you to feel more human.

Send a request for support. Open out to those close to you and tell them you need support. Make the most of every volunteer who offers to babysit. If you can sleep, take a nap, go to the movies, or get together with pals for coffee. It may also be beneficial to seek advice on parenting skills, such as caregiving techniques to improve your baby's sleep and ease fussing and screaming.

Remember that caring for your kid entails taking care of yourself.

Coping and Support

When depression occurs, the already stressful and demanding time after childbirth is exacerbated.

However, keep in mind that postpartum depression is never the fault of anybody. It is a prevalent medical condition that has to be treated.

If you're struggling to cope with postpartum depression, talk to your doctor. Inquire with your doctor or therapist about local support groups for new moms and women dealing with postpartum depression.

The sooner you seek treatment, the more prepared you will be to cope with depression while simultaneously enjoying your new baby.

Get ready for your appointment.

Following your first session, your healthcare provider may refer you to a mental health expert who will collaborate with you to create a treatment plan. Bring a trusted family member or friend to your session to help you recall everything.

What you can achieve

Prepare a list of the following things before your appointment:

Please describe any symptoms you've been experiencing and how long they've persisted.

All of your medical issues, both physical and emotional, including depression.

All prescription and over-the-counter medications, vitamins, herbs, and other supplements you use, as well as their amounts.

What questions should you ask your service provider.

Consider asking the following questions.

- What is the exact nature of my medical condition?
- What therapies are most likely to benefit me?
- What are the potential drawbacks of the remedies you propose?
- How fast do you anticipate my symptoms to improve with treatment?
- Is it safe to take drugs while breastfeeding?
- How long will I need treatment?
- What lifestyle changes will help manage my symptoms?
- How often should I schedule follow-up appointments?
- Does my risk of having other mental health concerns increase?
- Is it likely that this issue may arise if I have another child?
- What can I do to prevent this from occurring again if I have another child?
- Could you provide me with printed materials? What sites do you recommend?

Please do not hesitate to ask any further questions throughout your stay.

What to expect from your doctor?
Your doctor or mental health practitioner may ask you the following questions:

- What are your symptoms and when did they start?
- Have your symptoms improved or worsened with time?
- Do your symptoms make it harder to care for your child?
- Do you feel the same way about your kid as you expected to?
- Can you sleep whenever you want and get out of bed as needed?
- Describe your level of energy.
- Is your taste changing?
- How frequently do you experience nervousness, impatience, or anger?
- Have you ever contemplated harming yourself or your child?
- How much assistance do you get in caring for your child?
- Are there any other big pressures in your life, such as financial or marital issues?
- Have you had any other medical problems diagnosed?
- Have you ever received a mental health diagnosis, such as depression or bipolar disorder? If so, which therapy proved the most effective?

Depending on your replies, symptoms, and requirements, your doctor may ask more questions.

Making queries ahead of time can help you make the most of your visit.

Differential Diagnosis: PPD Versus Other Disorders

It is controversial whether a postpartum major depressive episode (postpartum depression [PPD]) differs sufficiently from prior major depressive episodes (severe depressive disorder) to merit a new diagnosis. In terms of epidemiology, etiology, and therapy, the evidence for and against the PPD diagnostic distinction is assessed. Overall, the evidence for distinguishing PPD from serious depressive disease is equivocal, and it is heavily impacted by how the postpartum period is classified. PPD may be distinct in the early postpartum period (variably defined, but typically with onset in the first 8 weeks), whereas depression in the later postpartum period may be more similar to a major depressive disorder occurring outside of the perinatal period, depending on symptom severity, heritability, and epigenetic data.

Given that PPD, the most frequent complication of delivery, is associated with immediate and long-term morbidity and mortality in both mothers and children, this idea has significant treatment implications. Future study on the difference between PPD and severe depressive illness should concentrate on the early postpartum period, when the fast decline in hormones adds to a withdrawal state that necessitates significant changes in central nervous system function.

For more than 150 years, experts have debated whether postpartum depression is sufficiently different from major depressive disorder to warrant designation as a separate diagnosis. In the mid-1800s, medical case studies started to distinguish between puerperal mental disturbances and nonpuerperal disorders. In the 1960s, a fundamental research described a form of "nonclassical depression" that included the vast majority of postpartum depressions. By 1994, the DSM-IV had incorporated a postpartum specifier for severe depression. Major depression "with postpartum onset" was a depressive episode that began within four weeks following delivery. This specifier continues in the DSM-5, however it now includes episodes that begin during pregnancy, "with peripartum onset."

Perinatal depression (PND) and postpartum depression (PPD) are frequently used interchangeably, but they mostly refer to substantial or minor depression that occurs during the pregnancy or persists for up to 12 months after birth. Aside from the start of the depressive episode, no classification considers PPD to be truly distinct from major depressive disease. Furthermore, the various definitions of PPD and PND differ on the amount of time that characterizes.

Throughout this review, major depressive disorder is used to describe a major depressive episode that occurs outside of the perinatal period (before pregnancy or more than 12 months after childbirth); in PPD studies, the reference period is clarified with respect to the number of weeks to months after childbirth.

Other systemic limitations in determining if PPD is distinct from major depressive disorder include differences in screening tools used to evaluate a major depressive episode and similarities between depressed symptoms and "normal" postpartum experiences.

Fatigue, sleep disturbance, and lack of appetite might be signs of infant care issues rather than melancholy. Efforts to develop screening and diagnostic processes that account for the overlap between depression symptoms and postpartum adjustment are hampered by the previously stated lack of clarity and consistency in defining the postpartum period. The Edinburgh Postnatal Depression Scale (EPDS), the most widely used self-report screening measure for PPD, has lower specificity and sensitivity to detect a major depressive crisis in the postnatal period (variably defined) than a major depressive crisis at any other time. In other words, the EPDS may be more successful than the PPD (for which it was intended) in diagnosing severe depression.

The EPDS was rated the best of 16 depression measures validated for use among postpartum women in terms of reliability, validity, sensitivity, specificity, brevity, and the variety of populations for whom the scale was validated. The ideal PPD self-report measure would include possible distinct PPD symptoms that are absent from major depressive disorder screening tools, weight symptoms that coincide with usual postpartum experiences, and high content validity and reliability. In the absence of more specific screening protocols, PPD is difficult to differentiate from the relatively common "baby blues" and clinical disorders with symptom overlap, such as generalized anxiety disorder, obsessive-compulsive disorder, and postpartum psychosis. As a consequence, although the field of psychiatry strives for precision medicine, there is still great disagreement in critical aspects of PPD research techniques, such as how the postpartum period is defined and PPD assessed.

Because psychiatric diagnoses before and during pregnancy are the strongest predictors of PPD, it is probable that PPD is physiologically and phenotypically distinct from major depressive disorder only in women who have their first and only mental episode during pregnancy. It is unclear if there is a "pure" PPD syndrome in which women have a severe depressive episode just during pregnancy, and this may be less clinically meaningful given that the great majority of PPD cases (78%) are relapses of major depressive disorder. Major depressive disorder is a frequently recurring condition, and women who have had major depressive disorder before having their first child are 20 times more likely to have postpartum depression. Furthermore, pre-pregnancy depression predicts a more severe postpartum depressive episode, suggesting that if pure PPD exists, it might be a subtype with milder depressive symptoms.

Nonetheless, these data show that subtyping PPD may be effective depending on whether the PPD episode is isolated (i.e., pure PPD) or occurs in conjunction with a prior prepregnancy severe depressive episode or other mental disease.

With these restrictions and concerns in mind, we examine current data that support or refute the distinctness of PPD as a diagnostic, concentrating on results from the preceding four years to complement Di Florio and Meltzer-Brody's outstanding work. The following evaluation compares and contrasts PPD and severe depressive illness in terms of epidemiologic and etiologic data, as well as potential treatment choices. This data is used to determine if PPD should be classified as a distinct condition and to provide recommendations for further study.

Epidemiology has similar prevalence patterns.

To directly compare the prevalence rates of PPD and major depressive disorder, we concentrate on studies that assess both conditions in the same cohort. Overall, research utilizing this technique suggest that the prevalence estimates for PPD and major depressive disorder are similar. In one research, the 12-month prevalence rate of major depression was not significantly different between women 0-12 months postpartum and women of reproductive age who were not in the peripartum period (10.2% vs. 13.1%). Another research found that the prevalence of PPD (measured 6 weeks after birth) and severe depressive disorder were comparable (8.9% vs. 13.6%).

The rates varied statistically. When the risk of depression in the postpartum period was adjusted for risk factors that were more prevalent in the non-postpartum women's sample, it actually became greater than the risk of depression outside of the perinatal window (the fluctuations in their findings could be explained by their relatively small sample size). These data show that PPD and severe depressive disorder are both likely to be common.

Differences.

In comparison to estimating the prevalence of major depressive disorder, estimating the prevalence of PPD requires additional considerations, such as defining the postpartum period window and determining whether to include women with a history of major depressive disorder and/or any other psychiatric disorders. While focusing on subgroups prevents generalizations to the larger population of postpartum women, it can be useful in identifying risks and developing targeted When studies that define the duration of the postpartum window in significantly different ways are combined, important etiologic differences between PPD subtypes, as well as the underlying incidence of PPD caused by biological and hormonal events of delivery, may be obscured.

Symptoms are similar.

PPD and major depressive disorder are both complicated diseases with symptoms present in some but not all depressed persons. Studies comparing PPD and major depressive disorder show that some symptoms, such as anxiety (defined as up to 6 weeks after delivery), aggressive obsessional thoughts (defined as up to 3 months after delivery), restlessness and agitation (defined as up to 3 months after delivery), and impaired concentration and decision making (defined as up to 3 months after delivery), are either more common or more severe in women with.

Differences.

When depression initially appears during the peripartum period, the clinical presentation of depressed symptoms differs. Notably, women who experienced depression after 8 weeks after giving birth were nearly four times as likely than women who had depression during pregnancy to have severe depression. When compared to women who had depression during pregnancy or 8-12 weeks after childbirth, these women were more likely to have an anxious anhedonia subtype of depression.

Although there is no clear link between PPD and severe depression, this research suggests that PPD with an early postpartum start might have substantial clinical aspects.

Important Considerations:

Women endure depression throughout both the perinatal and postpartum periods. Estimating PPD prevalence rates is difficult because to variances in assessment procedures (self-report questionnaires vs. clinician-administered interviews), postpartum period definitions, diagnostic equipment, and risk factors (e.g., prior history of depression). However, most studies that compare the prevalence rates of PPD and severe depressive disorder find that depression occurs at similar rates. Furthermore, although some studies have shown that specific symptoms are more frequent when depression initially arises, the symptoms of PPD and major depressive illness are same. Future epidemiology study should compare the incidence and symptomatology of PPD with early postpartum onset (i.e., within 8 weeks after birth) to PPD with late postpartum start and severe depressive disease.

The beginning

PPD and major depressive disorder are caused by biological (genetic, neurological, and hormonal) and psychosocial (stressor) elements, as well as their interactions (epigenetics).

PPD differs from major depressive disorder in terms of timing (following birth), type of psychosocial stressors (e.g., raising a newborn infant, relationship adjustments), and potential physiological underpinnings (dramatic rise in gonadal hormones accompanied by rapid withdrawal related to pregnancy and birth, respectively). PPD and serious depressive disorder have certain risk factors in common. In terms of genetic, hormonal, neurological, psychological, and epigenetic risk factors, this section compares and contrasts PPD with major depressive disorder.

Variables of Molecular Origin.

Similarities.

The majority of evidence suggests that PPD and severe mental disorder are genetically linked. According to one extensive research, the significant overlap in genetic risk factors (e.g., monoamine oxidase [MAO], catechol-O-methyltransferase [COMT], and 5HTT) between PPD and major depressive disorder may imply that the two disorders are fundamentally the same with a temporal difference. Genes implicated in reproductive and stressful hormone pathways (e.g., estrogen and glucocorticoid receptor genes) are associated with PPD and severe depression. PND patients and non-PND patients share almost two-thirds of their genetic variation.

Differences.

According to studies on twins and nontwin siblings, PPD is more heritable than severe depressive disorder.

The sibling research discovered 40% heredity for postnatal depression (defined as depression within a year after birth) and 32% heritability for non-PND. Because PPD occurs during pregnancy, the authors reasoned that it may be more homogeneous in terms of possible causes, and hence more heritable than depression that occurs elsewhere. Heritability studies, on the other hand, have experienced methodological challenges, rendering heritability comparisons less useful. Previous research, for example, compared individuals who reported at least one PPD episode (with or without subsequent major depressive episodes) against those who reported just major depressive episodes after delivery. This strategy was used to contrast women who reported postpartum and non-peripartum major depressive episodes with those who reported just non-peripartum major depressive episodes. A more robust test would compare the DNA of those with pure PPD to those with severe depression.

The onset of a significant depressive episode during the postpartum period determines how well genetics predict PPD. Two systematic evaluations found that genetics are more associated with PPD in the early postpartum period (within 6-8 weeks postpartum) than in the late postpartum era.

The short genotype of the dopamine transporter gene, for example, predicted PPD in the early stages (weeks 1-8) but not in the later stages (weeks 9-24). postpartum, whereas genetic variations of the glucocorticoid receptor and corticotropin-releasing hormone receptor 1 enhance the risk of PPD in weeks 2-8 but not in months 6-8, and low activity versions of MAO-A and COMT predict more depressed symptoms at 6 weeks but not 12 weeks postpartum. Depressive symptoms that appeared between 6 and 8 weeks postpartum had the greatest heritability of PPD in one research that linked the date of start with heritability estimates.

Hormone Components

Similarities.

Acute and persistent stress are commonly the causes of major depressive episodes. However, depending on the developmental timing, kind, and length of stress exposures, these exposures may have long-term consequences on HPA axis function, increasing the likelihood of depression in general. Similarly, sex, gonadal hormones, and reproductive status all have an impact on stress response throughout time. Both PPD and SAD patients have dysregulated HPA axis function, which is likely to play a role in depression onset.

Differences.

The hormonal changes that occur during the postpartum period are what define PPD. Although hormonal alterations may be a cause of PPD, no solid relationship between PPD and hormone levels has been shown, whether examined in absolute or relative terms. Rather, scientific data shows that a small proportion of pregnant women are particularly vulnerable to the significant hormonal swings that occur.

In one research, five out of eight women with a history of PPD had depressive symptoms when progesterone and estradiol were exogenously boosted and then quickly decreased (to mimic the hormonal changes associated with pregnancy and postpartum). In contrast, the control group (all women with no history of PPD) showed no increase in depressive symptoms despite undergoing the same hormonal manipulation and getting similar peripheral hormone levels. Women who are susceptible to PPD are more likely to have depressed symptoms following other hormonal changes, such as menopause and oral contraception. These data indicate that PPD is more prevalent in a group of women who are susceptible to the mood-destabilizing effects of reproductive hormone exposures and fluctuations, and that this subset differs physiologically from those who are solely prone to non-perinatal severe depressive episodes.

Neurological Factors Similarities.

PPD includes many of the same brain regions that are active in severe depression. PPD and significant depressive disorder, for example, are linked to decreased activity in reward-related brain regions (e.g., ventral striatum) in response to non-infant-related pleasant stimuli. Women with PPD demonstrated lower activity in reward-related regions in response to signals from their own babies, and the severity of the PPD corresponds with how much of this response is repressed.

Lower responsiveness in reward-related regions may explain how PPD might impede bonding with the newborn, since reward response to the baby is known to be crucial for mother-infant attachment.

Furthermore, PPD and severe depressive disorder are connected to comparable neurotransmitter systems, namely the serotonergic and gamma-aminobutyric acid (GABAergic) systems. In severe depression and PPD, serotonin receptor binding at the 5HT1A receptor is reduced to a similar degree (direct comparisons within the same study have not been conducted). According to the research, GABAergic system failure (e.g., decreased GABA levels in the brain, reduced expression and function of GABAA receptors) might be the cause of both severe depressive disorder and PPD. Low levels of allopregnanolone, a progesterone metabolite and potent GABAergic neurosteroid, are linked to PPD rather than severe depressive illness. According to animal studies, women with PPD may not have abnormal allopregnanolone levels, but rather poor GABAergic tonic inhibition restoration after delivery and rapid clearance of allopregnanolone.

Differences.

Individuals with PPD showed reduced activity in many brain regions than those with severe depression. PPD moms had a muted amygdala response to (non-infant-related) unpleasant stimuli, with more severe anxiety and depression symptoms leading to a higher blunting of amygdala activity. In one research of depressed mothers, reduced amygdala activity was associated with increased self-reported anger toward the baby. When compared to healthy mothers, depressed mothers responded less to their own infant's scream in brain regions involved in emotional response and control. Women with PPD showed decreased activation of critical corticolimbic neurocircuitry involved in emotional salience and threat processing in response to negative emotional stimuli and infant distress signals. This response might explain why PPD moms exhibit less maternal tenderness and greater hostility toward their babies than healthy mothers.

Factors influencing psychosocial health:
Similarities.

Psychosocial variables impact both PPD and major depressive disorder. PPD was linked to both perceived stress (for example, feeling overwhelmed) and long-term stress (for example, financial hardship, a lack of job stability or flexibility). in a detailed review. Chronic psychosocial stresses have also been associated with severe depression. Low social support acts as a stress buffer and has been linked to both PPD and severe depressive disorders.

Differences.

Childbirth and newborn care cause major psychological disorders throughout the postpartum period. A meta-analysis of PPD predictors revealed that childcare stress and infant temperament had moderate to high impact sizes, but unexpected or unplanned pregnancy had a modest effect size. PPD risk is also determined by the manner of employment. When compared to vaginal delivery, having a cesarean section (planned or emergency) raises the chance of PPD. Parenting-related psychosocial stress predicts PPD in the late postpartum period, but genetic and physiological variables predict it in the early postpartum period. Parenting stress, particularly at 6 weeks postpartum, was connected to PPD within 3-6 months.

Variables related to epigenetics, include interactions between genes and their environment
Similarities.
Despite the fact that few studies have combined biological and psy-

chosocial predictors of PPD, those that have found that early childhood stressors, abuse, and neglect, for example, are among the most powerful environmental risk factors for the development of PPD and major depressive illness, conferring risk in part through epigenetic changes. When the effects of epigenetics or gene-environment interactions are investigated, genetic influences on the risk of PPD and severe depressive disorders are usually observed.

Many of the most well-studied depression genes (for example, COMT, MAO-A, BDNF, and 5HTTLPR) show varying relationships with PPD depending on contextual variables such as stressful life events, socioeconomic status, and birth season. Some of the same gene-environment interactions and epigenetic changes have been identified as major depression risk factors.

Childhood stress, for example, may alter the expression and function of the glucocorticoid receptor, which is likely to affect both major depressive disorder and PPD. Carrying one or two copies of the serotonin transporter gene, for example, raises the risk of depression when exposed to stressful life events; similarly, carrying the short allele amplifies the negative impact of dissatisfaction with one's current partner and negative life events on postpartum depression symptoms.

Differences.

Although there is no evidence that gonadal hormone levels predict PPD, estrogen has been demonstrated to induce DNA methylation at estrogen-responsive genes, including TTC9B and HP1BP3. In blood samples taken during early pregnancy, DNA methylation at these genes predicted PPD with higher than 80% precision. Hormonal changes and estrogen signaling during pregnancy and delivery may cause epigenetic alterations that increase the risk of PPD. Another recent research discovered that women with both short alleles of the serotonin transporter gene and a considerable decrease in estradiol from the third trimester to the first week after giving birth had a higher risk of depression 6 weeks later. Given the significant and rapid increases in estrogen levels from pregnancy to postpartum, estrogen-driven epigenetic changes and estrogen-dependent mechanisms are more likely to induce PND than non-PND.

Important Factors To Consider

PPD and severe depressive illness may develop for a number of causes. The underlying processes are not always mutually exclusive, and they will almost likely interact to enhance the risk of PPD and severe depression. Estradiol and progesterone, for example, have a wide range of effects on brain neurochemistry, structure, and function, and both hormones affect various biological systems associated with PPD, including neurological function, thyroid function, HPA axis function, and immunological function. More research is required to determine if various PPD phenotypes exist, each with a unique collection of etiologies and biomarkers. At the time, no biomarkers are used in clinical settings to diagnose depression or differentiate between potential underlying causes of depression. Although early data shows that methylation of estrogen-responsive genes might be a biomarker for PPD, bigger sample numbers are needed to justify expenditures.

Depression in the postpartum (or even prenatal) phase might suggest a more severe problem. Early postpartum major depressive episodes tend to be driven by biological factors associated with hormonal shifts, but late postpartum major depressive episodes may be caused by psychosocial stresses. Although PPD and major depressive disorder share many of the same causes (shared genetics involving monoamines, stress and reproductive hormones, chronic psychosocial stressors related to a lack of social support, HPA axis dysregulation, blunted reward responsiveness, and interactions between the serotonergic system and the environment), some underlying mechanisms appear to be unique to PPD (sensitivity to changes in reproductive hormones, esophageal dysreflexi

Considerations for Treatment Similarities and Treatment Goals.

Treatment for PPD and severe depressive disorder focuses on symptom reduction, with symptom remission being the ultimate aim. Furthermore, both major depressive disorder and postpartum depression treatments aim to enhance quality of life and function at work and at home. PPD and major depressive disorder therapies should be practical and acceptable, with an emphasis on minimizing side effects and unfavorable outcomes.

Differences.

PPD develops throughout delivery and infant care, therefore PPD therapies aim to enhance mother care as well. Women with PPD had weaker bonds with their babies than non-depressed moms, with more disengagement and lower positive emotion. Maternal behavior adjustment is essential for ensuring good baby development outcomes, as well as mother role satisfaction and self-efficacy.

PPD has been related to delays in cognitive and socioemotional development in newborns, and research suggests that the quality of mother-infant connection effects developmental outcomes. As a consequence, the ideal PPD therapy would involve not just symptom alleviation, but also improved mother care and less developmental damage to children. Although treating severe depression in moms with older children improves child outcomes, infancy is a vital developmental time that emphasizes the necessity of meeting PPD treatment objectives.

The medication's compatibility with breastfeeding is an important consideration for PPD therapy, which does not apply to severe depression. Although the choice to breastfeed is ultimately up to the mother, the American Academy of Pediatrics recommends it since it helps both the mother and the infant. In postpartum treatment, it is crucial to assess medication pharmacokinetics in terms of both breast milk transit and neonatal exposure. In most situations, neonatal exposure to most antidepressants while breastfeeding is safe and has no negative effects (though possible long-term repercussions have not been investigated).

Sertraline is widely regarded as a first-line antidepressant for PPD due to the comparatively high number of studies that revealed no detectable drug in nursing babies. Switching from one antidepressant to an experimental medicine, on the other hand, is not advised for a woman who is stable on her current regimen due to the increased chance of recurrence. Nonpharmacological treatments include psychotherapy, bright light treatment, and transcranial magnetic stimulation (TMS), which do not expose the infant to medications. Breastfeeding women who have modest depression symptoms and are not a danger to themselves or others may benefit from psychotherapy alone. TMS and bright light therapy have shown limited effectiveness in the treatment of prenatal mood disorders and are potential research topics.

Traditional antidepressants have several properties.
Monoaminergic-based antidepressants, such as selective serotonin reuptake inhibitors (SSRIs), are recommended as first-line treatments for major depressive disorder and PPD, according to expert recommendations and randomized controlled trials (RCTs). Although fewer pharmacologic studies have been conducted for the treatment of PPD, drugs that have been shown to be therapeutic for major depressive disorder, such as sertraline, fluoxetine, escitalopram, fluvoxamine, bupropion, venlafaxine, and nortriptyline, seem to be useful for PPD.

Furthermore, the response and remission rates of PPD and MAD SSRIs are similar.

Differences.

A recent meta-analysis of antidepressant effectiveness and tolerability in major depressive disorder comprised 522 randomized placebo-controlled trials, whereas we only know of nine antidepressant RCTs for PPD, all of which employed SSRIs. Open label studies for non-SSRIs such as bupropion and venlafaxine have been completed. As a consequence, the evidence supporting antidepressant effectiveness in PPD is less compelling than for severe depression, especially for medications other than sertraline, which has attracted greater attention owing to its relative safety while nursing.

Despite RCT evidence supporting the use of SSRIs for PPD, a small study comparing the charts of 26 women with PPD and 25 women with major depressive disorder found that postpartum women had more severe depression, took longer to respond to treatment, and were more likely to require multiple antidepressants. The limited sample size and research methodologies (such as a retrospective record review of treatment-seeking women) restrict the results' generalizability. Finally, although there is evidence that antidepressants may improve mother role satisfaction, they do not seem to impact genuine maternal-infant bonds. This conclusion is consistent with previous studies indicating that PPD's impact on mother-infant relations might persist long after clinical remission.

Hormonal state may alter the reaction to antidepressants. In two studies, women who experienced PPD within four weeks after giving birth had the best sertraline responses. Given the limited sample size for this subset of individuals with early-onset PPD, these results should be taken cautiously. Because the early postpartum period is characterized by acute withdrawal of ovarian steroids, including allopregnanolone (a GABAA receptor modulating neurosteroid with antidepressant and anxiolytic effects), and because SSRIs have been shown to increase peripheral allopregnanolone levels, these drugs may be particularly effective in women whose symptoms are exacerbated by hormonal

Psychotherapy is comparable.

Many of the same therapies, including cognitive-behavioral therapy (CBT), psychodynamic psychotherapy, and interpersonal psychotherapy (IPT), work for both PPD and major depressive illness. Psychotherapy therapies may help avoid both major depressive illness and PPD.

Differences.

According to some research, some types of psychotherapy may be more useful depending on whether the treatment is for PPD or major depressive disorder. While data shows that PPD treatments with a stronger interpersonal component, such as IPT, are more effective than CBT, both CBT and IPT interventions may help prevent and cure severe depression. This disparity may be explained by the fact that PPD occurs in a social setting (taking on a new role as a mother while maintaining and modifying present interpersonal connections).

Mother-infant psychotherapy is a more specific approach for PPD, focusing on enhancing mother-infant connection. These interventions seem to be effective in terms of reducing depressive symptoms and maybe boosting infant attachment security. Although a systematic review found that both individual and mother-infant psychotherapy interventions reduced PPD symptoms, the effect sizes for improvements in mother-infant relationship quality and child development outcomes were smaller, implying that treating PPD is necessary but insufficient to have a significant impact on these outcomes.

Neuromodulatory therapies have several similarities.

Electroconvulsive therapy (ECT) and transcranial magnetic stimulation (TMS) are two effective neuromodulatory treatments for severe depressive illness. ECT remains one of the most successful psychiatric therapies, and it is thought to be more effective than antidepressants. TMS thorough reviews and meta-analyses for serious depression have also indicated large effect sizes. Although there is less research on PPD, it seems to react similarly to TMS and ECT.

PPD-Specific Therapies

Estradiol.

Hormone withdrawal is one of the (possible) neurobiological distinctions between major depressive disorder and postpartum depression, hence hormonal treatments have been tried to treat it. Although exogenous sex steroids have been used to treat severe depression, they tend to be most effective when a hypogonadal condition exists (as during perimenopause). Transdermal estradiol was shown to be beneficial in treating PPD symptoms in two small randomized controlled trials and one open-label investigation. Interestingly, the treatment group in two estradiol studies for PPD did not have substantially higher estradiol levels than the placebo group. This research implies that estradiol therapy may include regulating postpartum estradiol variations rather than addressing a deficiency. Estradiol is not presently recommended as a first-line therapy for PPD owing to a lack of evidence and the danger of thromboembolic consequences.

Allopregnanolone.

Progesterone and its neurosteroid metabolite, allopregnanolone, are quickly removed during delivery and have been identified as promising targets for PPD treatment. The substantial increase and drop in allopregnanolone levels during pregnancy and postpartum is known to affect GABAergic tone, albeit this process may be dysregulated in PPD women. The US Food and Drug Administration (FDA) has authorized brexanolone (Zulresso; Sage Therapeutics, Cambridge, MA), a synthetic form of allopregnanolone, for the treatment of moderate to severe PPD that begins no later than 4 weeks after delivery (160). The Zulresso Risk Evaluation and Mitigation Strategies program now provides it. There is presently minimal evidence on breastfeeding safety; however, published research indicates that infant exposure should be maintained to a minimum (1%-2% of the mother's weight-adjusted dosage).

Although the mechanism behind brexanolone's effectiveness for PPD is unclear, it has been demonstrated that controlling GABAergic tone via neurosteroid-mediated GABAergic inhibition is beneficial in reducing depressed symptoms. Despite substantial evidence that GABAergic dysregulation contributes to the pathophysiology of major depressive disorder (for recent reviews, see Maguire, Lüscher and Möhler, and Frieder et al), it is currently unknown whether neurosteroid preparations such as brexanolone are an effective treatment for major depressive episodes that occur outside of the postpartum. However, an oral form of allopregnanolone (Zuranolone; Sage Therapeutics, Cambridge, MA) is in phase III clinical trials. In a recent phase II clinical study of individuals with major depressive disorder, zaranolone was shown to be more effective than placebo at reducing depression symptoms at the main endpoint.

Important Considerations:

According to current research, the majority of successful PPD treatment options are similar to those often utilized for severe depressive disorder. SSRIs and psychotherapy are essential therapies in both groups. Brexanolone is the sole FDA-approved therapy for PPD at this time. Despite the fact that PPD and major depressive disorder respond to many of the same therapies, this should not be interpreted as proof of a similar etiology or pathology, since the same drugs are effective for a variety of diseases.

Antidepressants and psychotherapy may be effective because they may impact transdiagnostic neurobiological components associated with emotion regulation. Understanding the variations between the etiologies of PPD and major depressive disorder, on the other hand, is critical for developing a more tailored treatment strategy.

Despite the presence of GABAergic impairment in major depressive illness, PPD occurs in the setting of hormonal withdrawal. Treatment of PPD with GABAergic dysfunction may be more beneficial, particularly in the early postpartum period. Furthermore, since pregnancy involves considerable changes in interpersonal roles, IPT might be especially beneficial for PPD. Finally, mother-infant interventions might be the most effective way to address the particular issues of motherhood. To ensure that treatment choices are successful in lowering PPD symptoms, increasing mother role performance, and improving child outcomes, more research into these and other innovative strategies will be necessary.

Chapter 10

17 Signs of a Woman's Trust Issues and How to Address Them

I s it clear that a certain lady in your life has difficulty trusting you, despite the fact that you have done nothing to earn her distrust? This might indicate that she is experiencing trust difficulties, and you may not be the only one who suffers as a result of her distrust.

This chapter will teach you how to identify a lady with trust difficulties. Knowing these indications will help you understand how to establish trust with a lady. It may take some time and effort, but she will ultimately learn to trust you and others.

What exactly do trust issues imply?

The term "trust issues" refers to a mental condition in which a person has trouble trusting both individuals in their life and strangers.

When a woman has trust difficulties, she finds it difficult to trust others since her trust has already been breached. She may have lost her feeling of security and safety, so she expects the worst from everyone.

Lindsey M. Rodriguez and other writers did research that will teach you all you need to know about mistrust and trust difficulties. It highlights the link between trust, neurotic attachment, jealousy, and relational abuse.

17 Signs of a Woman Who Lacks Trust

Trust is one of the most fundamental attributes required for a relationship to succeed. When two people are in a relationship, they must trust each other for it to endure. However, if the partnership lacks trust, one spouse may struggle to believe the other, even if they are telling the truth.

Here are several indicators that a lady lacks trust.

1. She is cautious.

When women are too guarded, they might be identified as having trust difficulties. When it comes to you, you will notice that their protective instincts are on high alert. Even when the warning flags are evident, she always makes sure you're safe.

Furthermore, someone who lacks trust would constantly want to know where you are to ensure your safety. When her protectiveness becomes inconvenient, you may be certain she has trust difficulties.

2. She's wary of her family and friends.

Another symptom of a woman's trust difficulties is her inability to trust her relatives and friends. She seemed to be always preparing for the worst. Even when the signs are obvious, she does not think their motives are genuine.

A woman with a low degree of trust feels that blood relations and close friends should not be singled out as having ulterior motivations. As a result, whenever she engages with them, she keeps a safe distance to avoid being wounded.

3. She tries to avoid closeness.

When a lady refuses to get personal with you, it indicates a trust problem in the relationship. Sometimes the explanation is that she does not trust your motives.

She is terrified of showing vulnerability if she gets intimate with you. She is also aware that some people exploit vulnerable people.

As a result, she will be always on guard, avoiding personal situations to avoid getting injured. She may pretend to love you, but she finds it difficult to communicate her feelings since she is afraid of being close. This is one way to determine if a lady has trust concerns.

4. She draws up old grievances.

When your girlfriend brings up past arguments, you can know whether she is experiencing trust concerns. When she does this often, you'll notice that she still has doubts about the difficulties, even when they've been resolved.

She may communicate her doubts because she is dissatisfied with them. Such ladies are reminded of comparable issues since you may have faced them in the past. As a result, their choice on the previous circumstance will be strengthened.

5. She enjoys eavesdropping.

Snooping is one of the signs of trust concerns to watch out for. When a woman lacks trust, she begins to scrutinize everything out of the ordinary. If you remain out late for a few more minutes, she may want to hear every detail.

She may get enraged if you are evasive in your responses because you deny her the security of knowing the whole truth. Furthermore, if you do not provide her with all of the necessary facts, she may get too concerned.

6. She is always gazing at your phone.

When looking for signs of trust issues, one thing to look for is if she often goes through your phone. She will continuously check your phone to see if you have met a new person.

When she sees you talking with a new person, she may start asking more detailed questions about them. At this point, she may suspect you are cheating on her and seeks closure.

A woman who lacks trust will go through all of your social media interactions to see what you're up to online.

7. She's begun following you on social media.

One of the signs of a woman with trust issues is when she constantly monitors you online when she is not physically there with you.

A woman who lacks trust will most likely continue to engage in your social media posts across all platforms, and she may use Pet Names to demonstrate that she has a certain role in your life.

She may refuse to give you any breathing room online because she does not want anybody to replace her in your life.

8. She hates it when you leave without her.

One of the signs of a woman with trust issues is her want to accompany you everywhere. If you want to hang out someplace, she will make sure she is present.

Most of the time, this prevents you from meeting new people who may be potential partners. When she's with you in public, she makes sure she's all over you so no one can approach you.

9. She likes overthinking.

A woman with trust issues will overthink everything. When she discovers something surprising, she interprets it in several ways. If you don't clarify her thoughts, she'll keep pondering until she finds a suitable landing location.

Overthinking is one of the signs of a lady who lacks trust. This is why many individuals choose partners who can have in-depth conversations. Overthinking is less frequent in such relationships since their partners will tell them all they need to know.

10. She does not have steady relationships.

The incapacity of a woman to develop solid connections is one of the symptoms that she has trust difficulties. She was always reflecting on who was faithful to her and who was not. If any of them commits a mistake, she will probably terminate the relationship.

She will reject anybody with even the smallest hint of treachery from her network because she does not want to experience heartache.

11. She avoids commitments.

One way to determine if a female has trust difficulties is if she avoids commitment at all costs.

Someone who issues with trust recognizes that commitment exposes her vulnerability, and she may not be ready to share that aspect of herself with others. As a consequence, when she feels forced to commit to a relationship, she is more inclined to pull out.

12. She nurtures animosity.

Women who have trust concerns have often had their trust violated. As a consequence, even if they go above and above, they will struggle to trust others. Such women usually find it difficult to accept new members of their group because they do not want to repeat their bad experience.

So, if you gently offend her, she may hold a grudge since she believes you would likely repeat it.

13. She's an outsider.

Another symptom of a woman with trust issues is her preference to be alone rather than with others.

One possible reason for this is that she has understood that living alone reduces the probability of unsettling those who would violate her confidence. As a consequence, the fewer people she is with, the less likely it is that her trust will be eroded.

14. She is frightened of abandonment.

Women who lack trust are always terrified of being abandoned. They are always terrified of being cut off or abandoned in their relationships.

When they get an emergency or strange contact from their colleagues, spouse, boss, or others, they immediately assume the worst. As a consequence, they are always prepared to let go if they feel anything is amiss.

15. She focuses on others' weaknesses.

One of the signs of a woman who struggles with trust is her focus on other people's vulnerability. She may struggle to appreciate the good in others since she is likely too focused on the difficulties. Instead of playing to their strengths and forging stronger bonds, she would back down and cut them off.

16. She attempts to speak honestly.

A woman with trust issues may find it difficult to communicate openly and honestly with her lover.

She may suppress her emotions, ideas, and fears, believing that expressing them will lead to weakness and eventual betrayal. This lack of open communication may impede the development of emotional connections in the relationship.

17. She is always seeking for confidence.

People who struggle with trust may want frequent reassurance from their spouses. They want proof of their partner's love and dedication. This might be shown as repeated questioning like "Do you still love me?" or a demand for regular shows of affection to assuage their concerns.

Incorporating these extra clues into the text helps to provide a more complete picture of trust difficulties in relationships and how they appear in a woman's conduct.

Check out this research report by Abdul Gaffar O. Arikewuyo and others want to learn more about how a lack of trust impacts romantic relationships. The study's title is The Influence of Lack of Trust on Romantic Relationships.

Why do women struggle with trust? Seven explanations.

Women, like men, might have trust challenges for a number of reasons. Concerns regarding trust are often motivated by negative experiences, anxieties, or personal difficulties. The following are some of the most prevalent reasons why some women lack trust:

1. Betrayals from the past

When a past relationship is betrayed, it may cause long-term emotional scars. Adultery, dishonesty, and violating significant pledges are all forms of betrayal. Because the person fears experiencing the same loss and misery again, these events may produce trust concerns in future relationships.

2. Adversity as a Child

Childhood experiences have a huge impact on one's capacity to trust.

Childhood traumas such as neglect, physical or mental abuse, and parental desertion may all contribute to trust difficulties. Adults who have gone through these traumas may struggle to trust people because they are fearful of being wounded or rejected, which mirrors their previous experiences.

3. issues with self-esteem

Women with poor self-esteem may hard to trust because they question their value. They may think they are unworthy of love or respect, therefore they may be cautious of anybody who expresses interest in them.

When you have low self-esteem, it might be difficult to trust that others care about you.

4. Insecurity

Insecurity about one's looks, ability, or attitude may cause trust difficulties.

Insecure people may fail to determine if someone is attracted to them or interested in a relationship. They may be distrustful of other people's intentions, expecting that others will not find them persuasive.

5. Control difficulties.

Some individuals acquire trust difficulties as a result of a need for control in relationships. They are concerned about the unpredictability of their emotions, behaviors, and the future of the relationship. This need for control may breed mistrust since they struggle to believe that things will work out without their interference.

6. Attachment style

Attachment theory suggests that early childhood experiences with caregivers impact how people form ties in adulthood.

Women with an anxious attachment style may dread abandonment and cling to their relationships, which may lead to jealously and trust difficulties. Those with an avoidant attachment style may avoid emotional connection and have difficulty trusting others owing to emotional detachment.

7. Emotional baggage that has yet to be addressed

Unresolved emotional difficulties from earlier relationships, such as sorrow, trauma, or disagreements, might reemerge in new relationships. Unresolved emotions or unhealed traumas may cloud judgment and cause overthinking or distrust, making it difficult to fully trust a new relationship.

When dating a lady with trust difficulties, keep in mind that trust problems are diverse and may be impacted by a mixture of these variables.

Working through trust difficulties often include self-reflection, engagement with one's partner, and maybe seeking the assistance of a therapist to address the root reasons and develop skills for restoring trust in current relationships.

9 strategies to assist a lady who has trust concerns.

If you're wondering how to date someone who suffers with trust, one method to assist them is to communicate honestly.

When you know what to do, helping a lady with trust difficulties is simple. Jessica Riley's book accomplishes just that. Reading Trust Issues teaches partners how to cope with anxiety, insecurity, and jealousy in their relationships.

Meanwhile, here are some things you may do to assist a lady dealing with trust:

1. Be frank and honest.

Create a trustworthy atmosphere by communicating openly and honestly. Share your emotions, opinions, and experiences with her. Show that you are open to discuss any issues she may have. This openness sets an excellent model for her to follow when it comes to developing trust.

2. Listening attentively

Active listening requires not just hearing what she says, but also understanding her emotions and anxieties. Empathy and affirmation, such as "I understand why you feel that way," might help her feel noticed and appreciated.

3. Maintain her limits.

Understanding and respecting her limits is critical. Respect her need for space or time to process her feelings, and recognize any boundaries she establishes on discussion subjects. This act of respect demonstrates your care for her comfort and well-being.

4. Consistency

Do you want to know how to assist someone who is dealing with trust?

Consistent conduct and deeds build confidence. Keep your words and actions trustworthy and constant. Keep your pledges and responsibilities, and she will know she can rely on you.

5. Help her heal.

Encourage her to seek professional therapy if her trust concerns are due to prior trauma or unresolved emotional baggage. Offer to assist you discover a therapist or counselor who specializes in trust difficulties and emotional recovery.

6. Reassurance

She needs reinforcement in order to feel secure in her relationship. Frequently convey your love and dedication to her. Reaffirm your commitment to make the partnership work, particularly during difficult times.

7. Try not to get defensive.

When addressing trust concerns, avoid becoming defensive or dismissive. Instead, engage in discussions with empathy. Recognize her sentiments as legitimate, even if you disagree with them. Avoid blaming or disputing, since this might worsen trust concerns.

8. Please bear with us.

Trust takes time to develop, so be patient as she grows to trust you. Recognize that her questions and fears are normal. Allow her the time and space she needs to develop trust in her own manner.

9. Collaboration is crucial.

Building trust requires a collective effort. Talk about your relationship freely and honestly. Address her concerns and collaborate to create solutions. This collaborative effort may foster a feeling of security as well as a shared commitment to establishing trust.

So, how do you handle trust issues?

Remember that assisting someone with trust difficulties is a process that may include setbacks. Continue to show your commitment to her and the relationship. If trust difficulties continue and have a negative impact on the relationship, seek expert assistance to navigate and address the root causes.

Questions & Answers

To have a better understanding of a woman's trust concerns, explore the following key questions:

What leads females to be distrustful?

Girls' trust difficulties are often the result of past betrayals or traumas, such as adultery, emotional abuse, or abandonment. Childhood trauma and poor self-esteem might also be contributors. These characteristics influence their willingness to trust in future relationships, leading to skepticism.

How do you deal with a gal who is suspicious?

Patience, open communication, and understanding are required while dealing with a distrustful woman. Establish trust by speaking the truth, actively listening, and respecting limits.

Encourage her to get professional assistance if needed, comfort her, and work together to develop trust.

Is it possible to love someone while also distrusting them?

It is possible to love someone yet struggle to trust them. Trust concerns may strain a relationship, yet love can exist alongside them. Restoring trust in a relationship requires communication, consistency, and reassurance.

Should I date an untrustworthy woman?

It is feasible to date a woman who suffers with trust, but it requires empathy, patience, and a desire to assist her. Examine your commitment to assisting her recuperation and establishing trust. If trust difficulties are interfering with your relationship, get expert help.

Should you remain in a relationship if you do not trust your partner?

Maintaining a relationship without trust may be difficult. Trust is the cornerstone of all strong relationships. If trust concerns continue and attempts to repair trust are futile, it may be important to reconsider the relationship's sustainability and seek counseling or therapy.

Simply stated,

After reading this essay, you should be able to recognize the indications of a distrustful lady. When you see she has trust concerns, offer her compassion and sensitivity. Tell her you understand her predicament and want to help her better it.

Understanding and dealing with women's trust difficulties is a difficult and sensitive task. Recognizing the indications of trust difficulties is the first step towards creating a helpful and empathetic atmosphere. Trust difficulties may arise as a consequence of a variety of events, with the underlying reasons firmly established in past traumas, anxieties, and attachment patterns.

Handling trust difficulties needs patience, honest communication, and a dedication to trust restoration. It is vital to remember that trust difficulties do not define a person, and that healing and development are achievable with the correct help and knowledge.

Finally, creating a secure and trustworthy relationship is a shared duty that may lead to a more intimate and meaningful connection between couples.

5 Ways to Deal with a Paranoid Partner.

Being in a relationship is a difficult endeavor. To create a relationship, you must work hard, trust, be honest, believe in one another, and love.

Everyone is unique, and for a relationship to work, both sides must accept each other as they are. Sometimes a couple gets along just well, yet one of their characteristics might strain their relationship.

Paranoia is one of these characteristics. So, how would you cope with a paranoid partner?

Consider that your spouse need reassurance from time to time, listens in on every discussion, questions your conduct, and often lacks faith in you. While it is tempting to disregard these issues, repeated behaviors have the ability to ruin everything.

Chapter 11

Real-Life Stories of Those Who Overcame PPD

Hello, and welcome to our universe. Survivors of perinatal mood and anxiety disorders, including postpartum depression, have made the decision to have another child. Some of us have made great progress, while others continue to wait. You will discover more about it later. For the time being, I'd want you to take a seat, relax, and maybe even have a cup of tea before meeting the people that altered my life.

Amy Brannan is a well-known actress.

Amy has a four and a half-year-old daughter and intends to adopt another. She and her spouse have been married for five years and reside in Washington state. Amy's remarks appear below.

I saw nothing until my kid was five months old. I consulted many physicians because I suspected something was wrong, but no one suggested postpartum depression, which remains the most hardest for me to accept. I eventually began doing my own research and discovered a PPD website that documented each symptom.

My husband and I visited the doctor in 2008, and I was diagnosed with postpartum depression, anxiety, and OCD tendencies.

I began therapy and medication when my kid was 10 months old. This went on for 2.5 years. In late 2010, I wasn't getting better, and I felt trapped, as if I was nearly over the hump. I was suggested to consult a psychiatrist, who was really helpful.

I also started looking for ladies who have/had postpartum depression, which is when I came across PPD blogs and saw the light at the end of the tunnel.

Facebook, PPDChat, and this network of surviving mothers saved my life and sanity, enabling me to accept my situation and assist others. In order to begin writing as a kind of self-treatment, I launched my own PPD survivor's blog. I still cope with the anxiety and sadness induced by PPD, but it is no longer PPD. We decided not to get pregnant again due to the severity of my postpartum depression, therefore we are now on the waiting list for our next kid! That was the most hardest choice I had to make: not to get pregnant again while feeling devastated, inadequate, and a failure.

I'd want to reassure ladies that everyone's journey is unique, and each woman will have distinct symptoms. I'd want to reassure women that they are not damaged or weird, nor are they failures as moms or spouses. I am evidence that guilt may be a very negative aspect of PPD. I'd want to talk about "not" becoming pregnant again after PPD, and how women make that choice. I really wanted to read about it, and I couldn't find anything last year when I was struggling the most.

I want to be able to reach out to other women who, like myself, sought treatment when they thought they had hit rock bottom. Women who are unsure of what is wrong with them and feel alone. I wish to support and encourage their families, particularly their spouses. I couldn't have done it without my loving and supportive hubby.

Deborah Rimmler.

Deborah is a mother of two sons and a wife. Please meet Deborah.

In this series, I'd want to share what we found as a group and individually as we worked to build a new postpartum experience for ourselves and our families. I'm hoping we can contact any mothers who are considering having a kid after giving birth. Those who have successfully had a vaginal birth after a c-section, or VBAC. We are "BAPPD" (Baby After PPD) survivors seeking to promote hope.

Mrs. Grace Parsons

Grace and her husband have been married for eight years. They have a 3 ½ year old son and a newborn child born in October 2011. She is an Oregon native who has been living in Mexico since 2006. Grace is a friend of mine.

From December 2008 until September 2010, I had the most severe postpartum depression and anxiety. I'd want to discuss my experiences with postpartum approaches that have helped me stay healthy so far with my second child, communicating with your spouse, prenatal medications, and self-care. I hope we can reach out to mothers suffering from PPD and provide them hope for recovery and healing. I also hope that mothers who are contemplating having another child feel encouraged and empowered to do so. You can recover!

Kate Ferguson

Kate, a married lady with two children, lives in the United States. She suffered PPA/PPD after her first pregnancy. Here's Kate, my real-life pal.

I had danger indications and sought assistance, but it was difficult to locate. It is too tough. That transformed my life, both professionally and emotionally. I prepared for and had a good pregnancy and postpartum time with my second kid. Six months later, feeling better, I returned to a job I had abandoned during my postpartum depression. My profession include counseling and advocating for PPD mothers. Everything comes full circle and is quite fulfilling.

I wish to increase awareness of risk factors and urge others to get treatment. Furthermore, it would be useful to underline all of the many ways we choose to manage pregnancy following PPD and how valid each was/is. I want to reach out to women who think they don't like being a mother, as well as lost loved ones who don't understand what's wrong and aren't getting treatment.

I'd always wanted three children. My next kid is due on May 3, 2012, so I'm diving back in with my eyes wide open.

Suzanne Stanard

Suzanne is a mother of two sons. She conquered postpartum depression and anxiety with her first child, but she is just now coming out of it with her second. She's originally from North Carolina. Let me introduce Suzanne.

When I had my first kid, one of the most essential things I learned was the need of getting assistance if you suspect anything is wrong.

I waited longer than I wanted to admit, but once I made the first step, the relief was instantaneous. I was lucky not to have PPD/A the second time because of some significant preparation (we all understood what to look for). I really hope that this series will allow us to reach out to women who have suffered from a prenatal mental disorder and are afraid to have another child as a result of their experience. It is terrifying. However, it may also be fantastic.

Yuz Yuz Rozenblum now lives in Melbourne, Australia. She has been married for four years and has had three pregnancies and two children, both delivered at 36 weeks weighing just over 2kgs and both with feeding issues, the second worse than the first, and has subsequently been diagnosed with laryngomalacia (floppy larynx). Yuz's statements often elicit laughter and, on rare instances, tears.

At 36 weeks, my daughter was delivered unexpectedly. After the delivery, we were separated, and she remained in the hospital for five days after I was released. When my daughter was five weeks old, I was formally diagnosed with PPD (postnatal depression or PND in Australia) and PPA (PNA), and I was admitted to a parent-infant unit at a mental health institution (which I lovingly referred to as the nuthouse) for three weeks. For the following nine months, I went to the nuthouse on a regular basis and became a part of their outreach program, which included a staff person visiting my home every two weeks to check how I was doing.

In the middle of 2010, we decided to have another child, and I became pregnant shortly after. Our son was delivered at 36 weeks by planned c-section after a challenging pregnancy (bi-partite placenta, placenta previa, and vasa previa, the latter of which gave my child a 20% chance of survival if my membranes broke suddenly). I was taken to the hospital at 34.5 weeks, had a planned c-section at 36 weeks, and was discharged five days later with my husband. My kid was readmitted to the hospital after a week and a half, with only a 50g weight increase, and stayed for nine weeks until being (eventually) diagnosed with laryngomalacia (floppy larynx) at 11 weeks. I followed him to the hospital for the whole of his stay.

My purpose for sharing my story is to show other postpartum depression (postnatal depression) survivors that a happy result is achievable. It is not your fault if you have a perinatal mood or anxiety problem;

you did not ask for it, and it is not permanent. The fact that we had a poor time the second time around was unrelated to my emotional condition. My love and dedication to my kid have never faltered. On a more practical note, I'd want to be prepared to discuss where and how you may receive the assistance you need in Australia. We have wonderful tools and a fantastic medical system that make it easy to seek and get the assistance you want without having to take out another mortgage. On an emotional level, I would urge mothers to make plans ahead of time to increase their chances of having a positive experience.

My daughter was the catalyst for my diligent preparation. I didn't want her to see me struggle through an even more tough transition phase on top of having a brother.

My second driving ambition was to free my husband from the burden of caring for a toddler, a baby, and an ailing wife.

Amber Koter-Puline, a working mother of two, works part-time. Amber's first kid was born in 2007, and she had a significant postpartum reaction. Since she recovered with appropriate treatment and care, her primary emphasis has been to assist and educate expectant and new moms about the postpartum period and being a first-time mom. Amber is responsible for new mother and postpartum support services in the Atlanta region. She resides in Atlanta with her husband and two boys.

After overcoming a perinatal mood or anxiety disorder while pregnant with her second son, Amber wanted to form a network of parents who could support one another throughout pregnancy, trying to conceive, or adoption. This event was really beneficial to her.